Masters
of cinema

Clint
Eastwood

Clint Eastwood in *Unforgiven* (1992).

Contents

Introduction

The actor, star and filmmaker Clint Eastwood has not always found favour with the critics. For long periods of time, media and press alike have ignored his work, holding it in a certain contempt and considering it at best suspect, and at worst, something not to be associated with. Seemingly born under the same sign as the subversive Sergio Leone westerns, the impassive Eastwood certainly hasn't helped matters. His controversy-courting role in *Dirty Harry* is a case in point. But Eastwood is a determined character who has never stopped working, and in fact, has never stopped capturing the public's imagination or exploring new areas. Like his character in *The Outlaw Josey Wales*, Eastwood's long career has seen countless conversions and U-turns on the part of the critics. And today, while his films have garnered numerous awards and he is unanimously praised for a twenty-five-year body of work as large as the American continent, Eastwood's films still risk eliciting a negative response. His films, now recognized universally, are often too quickly understood, their mastery regarded as so self-evident that they require no further discussion. Considered 'classic' films, they are associated with a certain kind of clarity, transparent meaning and immediate readability. But one should not put one's trust so easily in the filmmaker's art. He has often worked hard to hide his deepest motives and the often subtle and secret meanings of his films. Actually Eastwood's films plumb the depths. He is a tireless archaeologist in search of treasure, always digging and dreaming of the day he might uncover the hidden heart of human nature. In *Blood Work*, Eastwood plays a criminal profiler, who conducts his own inquiries at crime scenes, playing and replaying video footage until another hidden meaning finally emerges and lifts the veil of illusion. In the same way, the truth about this particular filmmaker can only be found within the films themselves. But of course, this in turn will become a never-ending quest, an illusion of perception of which we have already been warned: 'Sport, truth, like art, is in the eye of the beholder. You believe what you choose and I'll believe what I know.'[1]

Clint Eastwood on the set of *Absolute Power* (1997).

What is an Image?

From *A Fistful of Dollars* to *Escape from Alcatraz*

Clint Eastwood in Sergio Leone's
A Fistful of Dollars (1964).

'I went into Mattson's, a sport shop up on Hollywood Boulevard here, and bought some black Levis and bleached them out, roughed them up. The boots, spurs and gun belts I had from *Rawhide*; the hat I got at a wardrobe place in Santa Monica. The little black cigars I bought in Beverly Hills. The poncho I got in Spain.'[2]

Ten years after he left Hollywood for Italy to make the low-budget western *A Fistful of Dollars* (1964), this is what Eastwood said about how he created his character's appearance. The film's iconic images of Eastwood signalled a whole new mythology about the actor, right down to the cigarillos and poncho — his cult objects in the film, now as recognizable as Charlie Chaplin's cane and shoes, Marilyn's white dress or James Dean's T-shirt. Although the film was to also see Eastwood emerge as a new kind of icon and star — perhaps the most famous of the decade — it is worth remembering that at the time journalists did not take Eastwood seriously as an actor (although by then he had already appeared in fifteen films and over 200 episodes of *Rawhide*), let alone a director . One of the paradoxes of Eastwood's career was that he had to go to Italy in order to attract a following in his own country. His appearance in Sergio Leone's *Dollars* trilogy of films[3] was to also mark the beginning of a tortuous path at the hands of the critics, whose vehemence against him in the 1970s would only be rivalled by the sheer intensity of their turnaround and consequent adulation for his works in the 1990s and beyond. With a ground-swell of silent support among American audiences but looked down on by America's East Coast, Eastwood would always be aware of and explore this gap, the distance between the image he projected and the image others would project back about him. Right from the beginning of his career to the end of the 1970s, it was this gap that preoccupied him and he worked tirelessly from film to film to bridge it.

Going with the flow

Born on 31 May 1930 in San Francisco, California, to a father of English and Scottish heritage and a mother with Dutch and Irish origins, Clinton Eastwood, Jr came into the world just as America tipped into the Great Depression. The result of the Great Crash on Wall Street's stock markets, with huge drops in share prices on 24 and 29 October 1929, it set off a snowball effect in the U.S. economy. The country underwent a massive collapse in consumption and production, and the stock markets entered a period of chaos as agricultural prices dropped, bankruptcy and mass redundancies piled up and the nation entered a state of shock accompanied by an era of soup kitchens.[4]

In his own personal way, Eastwood later explored the suffering that plagued America's anonymous towns and rural areas during this difficult period,[5] in films like *Honkytonk Man* (1982), the final journey of a country-and-western singer, inspired, according to the filmmaker, by what he witnessed as a boy around him and in his family photo albums. But the Eastwood family never experienced the extreme poverty of the Depression-era towns, nor that of America's agricultural smallholders forced to leave their land in search of food. At the end of the 1920s, Eastwood's father was a bonds salesman and although, given the financial crisis, that could seem like one of the Laurel and Hardy comedies of the time (James W. Horne's *Big Business*, 1929, where Stan and Ollie play Christmas tree salesmen in summer), it does indicate that Clint Eastwood was born into a middle-class home. The Eastwoods may have been set adrift by the financial crisis and left without any savings, but as far as the filmmaker can remember, he did not suffer any deprivation as a child, although, even then, he took refuge in day dreams and a vivid imaginary life. This proved to be another aspect of his childhood that was to later precipitate various fictional explorations. The motif of a boy looking out of a window into another world is presented in the films *Honkytonk Man* and *A Perfect World* (1993); that of a young girl all alone in a forest is shown in *Pale Rider* (1985); a forlorn woman is presented in *The Bridges of Madison County* (1995). Essentially, all these characters dream of some figure appearing on the horizon to take them away, releasing them from boredom and offering them the promise of another world.

In reality, the Eastwood family spent the 1930s drifting around California, the young Clint attending no less than eight schools. With each new relocation, the precious piano bequeathed to the family by Clint's paternal grandmother was moved too, as Eastwood's sometimes-absent, sometimes-present father searched for temporary work in Piedmont, Oakland, Spokane, Redding (Northern California), then back to Oakland, Pacific Palisades (Los Angeles), Sacramento, Glenview, before finally going back again to Piedmont where the family at last found some stability for a time. It is clear that

Below and opposite page:
Clint Eastwood at Universal Studios
in the 1950s.

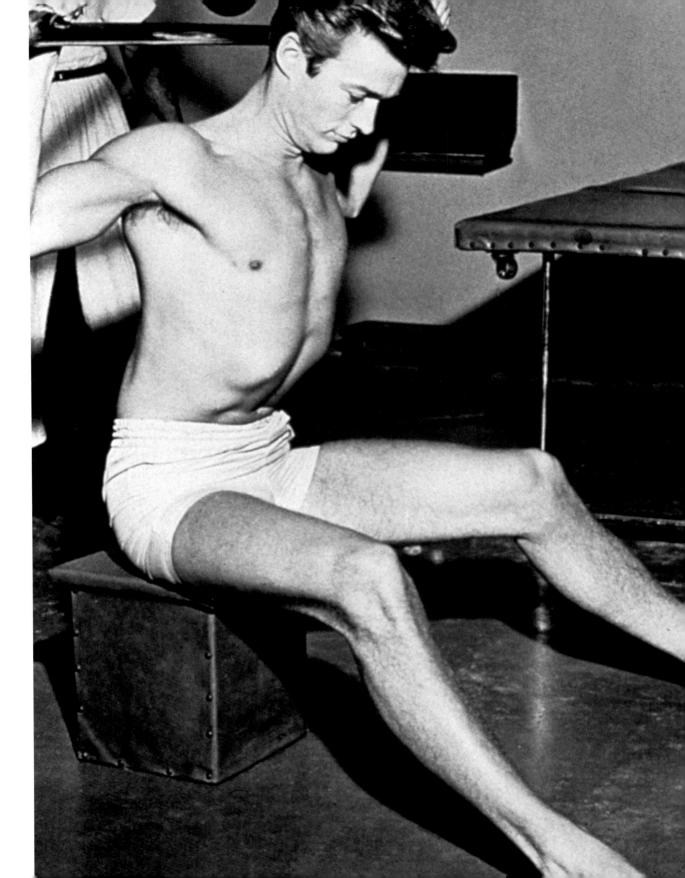

Eastwood's early life had a formative effect on him. The young boy was obliged to follow a path and direction that was not his own. It created in him an ideal about a happy, unified family, which was later to be extended out into a group, even a community. Later in his life he would always ensure he was in control and able to impose his desires on the world around him, as opposed to being buffeted by forces external to him.

By adolescence, Eastwood had grown into a tall and handsome young man but he was shy almost to the point of introversion (perhaps this characteristic might be at the root of his later laconic manner?). As well as what must have been the thrill of his first acting experiences at Piedmont Junior High School and the discovery of a country music[6] bar in Springfield, one particular experience seems to have singularly marked the young Eastwood in the latter half of the 1940s. The concert, from the 'Jazz at the Philharmonic' series, at the Oakland Auditorium in 1946, featuring Coleman Hawkins, Flip Phillips, Lester Young and Charlie 'Bird' Parker, made Eastwood want to become a musician. Although Eastwood would have almost certainly been listening to records by Art Tatum and Fats Waller at the time, this concert proved to be a pivotal point in his life. It heralded a before and after moment: experiencing Charlie Parker.

A jazz musician whose self-assured and instinctual playing embodied cool effortlessly, it showed the young Eastwood how impatience, social rage and irrepressible energy could be sublimated into an art form. Still impressionable and unable to articulate the silent stirrings in his own being after this first experience of Parker, until the mid-1950s Eastwood went with the flow, drifting a bit and exploring his sensations, passively reacting to anything that crossed his path. After 'Bird' and because of jazz and bebop, in 1951 he also dreamed about entering Seattle University's music department. However, the start of war in Korea altered his plans and forced him to attend military training at Fort Ord, Monterey. He became a lifeguard at the camp's pool and it was here that he first crossed paths with various young actors who suggested that he too consider acting because of his notable good looks. Nothing tangible as yet, but 1953 saw Eastwood enrolling at the Los Angeles City College, officially to study 'business

administration'. But he spent most of his time in the drama department and, as one thing led on from another, he eventually made various useful contacts (such as cinematographer Irving Glassberg and the director Arthur Lubin) that brought about a first screen test, at the Hollywood studio Universal in 1954. Eastwood was horrified by the results and barely recovered from seeing himself on film for the first time: 'I thought I was an absolute clod. It looked pretty good; it was photographed well, but I thought, "If that's acting, I'm in trouble."'[7] He spent the next few years 'correcting' his film acting, ridding himself of what he thought were unnecessary gestures. He was to continue doing this — initially with Sergio Leone and then later on his own — using a minimalist style, adopting a poker face and being economical with his physical actions — to such an extent that even later in his career the critics attacked him, accusing him of not really acting properly, as well as a whole host of other things they saw as wrong in his films.

The man without a face

Despite Eastwood's reservations, Universal-International was satisfied with the screen test and offered the young actor a contract starting 1 May 1954 and finishing at the end of October the following year. It was a standard studio contract, paying $75 a week and aimed at nurturing the young talents the studio

Opposite page: Clint Eastwood and Tab Hunter in William A. Wellman's *Lafayette Escadrille* (1958).

Right: William A. Wellman's *Lafayette Escadrille* (1958).

routinely took on, in the hope that one day some would bloom. At that time the studio had a veritable school or 'stable' aimed at developing protégés into professional actors, putting them through a rigorous schedule of daily acting classes, sport, exercise and some initial appearances in studio films. During this time, Eastwood avidly read *To the Actor*, by the great actor and iconoclastic disciple of Stanislavski's Method, Mikhail Chekhov (1891−1955). Eastwood's teachers of the period described the young man as a conscientious student — perhaps a way of saying he was a little gauche but diligent. The novice actor enjoyed life at a big studio and, unlike a lot of his peers, remained constantly curious, always asking questions and hanging around the sets, becoming more interested in the work of the directors than the actors. At the end of 1954 he landed his first part, as a lab assistant in a scene in *Revenge of the Creature* (1955) directed by Jack Arnold. A few other films followed, as well as a more difficult period after his contract ended with Universal. He appeared in a small number of bit parts, with sometimes a few lines — rarely more and often less. At

one point he even played against Francis the Talking Mule in Arthur Lubin's *Francis in the Navy* (1955). At the start of his career, Eastwood's roles varied from the part below the supporting actor to the man in the background. In short, he was getting somewhere but nowhere very much, and he was not making an impact. Of his first films at Universal, only Jack Arnold's *Tarantula* (1955) is memorable, in which he plays a jet pilot, whose face is concealed by a helmet. It curiously foreshadows one of his later starring roles — in *Firefox* (1982) — but it also provides a fitting symbol for his career at this point: Clint Eastwood, the man with no face. Later in his life, with some distance and a modicum of detachment about his early years, the filmmaker and actor was able to put his finger on what it was about him in relation to the 1950s, then celebrating a new-found prosperity and 'the American way' against the backdrop of the Cold War: he just did not have the look the decade required.[8]

Eastwood as a young actor had to undergo the relentless studio system, the Hollywood dream factory and its manufacturing of 'stars', a production line which 'rationalizes, standardizes, sorts, eliminates any defective pieces, moulds, assembles, manufactures, polishes and embellishes, in short, a perfect star-making machine'.[9] But his physical appearance resisted this kind of treatment, this type of moulding and standardization. And the decision makers during this more conformist era found his voice too soft, his Adam's apple too prominent, his teeth too obvious, and his gaze too unflinching. Even his height seemed to hark back to another era of actors like Gary Cooper, Henry Fonda and James Stewart. In fact, the unique features that set him apart and were eventually to lead him to fame were exactly the things that blocked his path in the 1950s. So much so that when he did belatedly become a star as a result of the spaghetti westerns, it was entirely an accident of fate, totally unexpected and, most importantly, he had remained a completely unmanufactured 'phenomenon', not part of the Hollywood system that was to take a long time to recognize his uniqueness. His appearance on screen was to ultimately herald an original kind of film presence, a manifestation of a new kind of heterogeneity that the Hollywood of the late 1950s and early 1960s had failed to pick up on and make use of. The coming of Eastwood represented the coming of a new kind of physical presence on screen: the arrival of the modern body. In order to get to this point, Eastwood was to have to take a detour and work in TV, which, unlike his film career at the time, gave him valuable time to develop, allowing him to create a preliminary image that he would have to rid himself of just as quickly and violently in order to be free of its constraints.

'The most handsome cowboy in the world'

The opportunity for Eastwood that was provided by a part in CBS TV's *Rawhide* series in 1959 needs to be understood within a particular historical context. The 1950s proved to be such a boom time for TV that it actually became of serious concern for the Hollywood studios, who worried they were losing a whole new generation of filmmakers, scriptwriters and actors willing to work in the new creative space TV offered them. Eastwood was not to be the only person who used TV drama serials as a chance to get on screen.[10] And like many serials of the time, *Rawhide*, which ran from January 1959 to December 1965, also had ambitions for the western,

Opposite page and below:
Clint Eastwood in *Rawhide* (1959–65).

taking up the baton of what was then the ruling genre in Hollywood. It reached its zenith at the end of the 1950s and the beginning of the 1960s (John Ford's *The Man Who Shot Liberty Valance*, 1962), but was now at risk of being so eclipsed by TV that Hollywood producers blamed TV and later, even more virulently, the spaghetti westerns themselves for reducing the genre's currency by saturating it with a surfeit of forms. In fact, these new creative offerings ensured the genre's survival, even the critical renewal of its epic form, which was at risk of extinction at the time.

The irony of this context was that Eastwood, given a permanent part in the series from the outset, now found he had front-row seats to observe the secrets of the Hollywood image factory. In fact it provided a better opportunity than his time at Universal. Over the weeks, months and years, the TV serial became a formative basis for Eastwood's career. For a start, he was able to meet the movie stars invited onto the series to enhance particular episodes (Barbara Stanwyck, Peter Lorre and so on). He also had fixed hours and times to work, giving him time to perfect the job of acting, if not its art. And, above all, *Rawhide* provided him with an opportunity to observe a broad range of different directors at work on each of the episodes — spanning the good and the bad, as well as high-profile

Above: Clint Eastwood in Sergio Leone's *A Fistful of Dollars* (1964).

Below: Clint Eastwood and Silvana Mangano in Vittorio De Sica's *Una sera come le altre* (1967).

Opposite page: Clint Eastwood and Lee Van Cleef in Sergio Leone's *For a Few Dollars More* (1965).

Following pages: Eli Wallach and Clint Eastwood in Sergio Leone's *The Good, the Bad and the Ugly* (1966).

Hollywood directors at the ends of their careers. He also dreamed of directing an episode himself, but as every dream has a downside, the lucky break *Rawhide* represented also meant he was prohibited as an actor in the show from directing an episode, or taking any other roles, because of a possible 'conflict of interest with the sponsors'. There was also a demanding old-fashioned routine to deal with and a cheaply constructed set of the Wild West. And finally his character: Rowdy Yates, a handsome and wholesome young man without any trace of a dark side, who only ever rebelled in a limp, half-hearted way, spending most of the time obeying orders. While the actor's first fans saw him as 'the most handsome cowboy in the world', Eastwood nicknamed his character 'the idiot of the prairie'.

Clearly, these factors eventually prompted the actor to blindly accept, in 1964, the offer of a role from a practically unknown Italian director. *The Magnificent Stranger* (later re-titled *A Fistful of Dollars*), the first of Sergio Leone's trilogy, offered Eastwood a role that was essentially a dark negative of Rowdy Yates. The Man with No Name was a grown-up cowboy; dirty, crafty, individualistic, adept and minimalist in his responses, practically mute, violent at will and getting a kick out of it too. Eastwood also made the joyful discovery of Leone's filmmaking style, a scathingly jubilant and absolute response

to the neat aesthetics of *Rawhide*. Undoubtedly Eastwood's frustration towards his career was raising its head once again. It was to find an outlet in Leone's films, which offered Eastwood a chance to move on from his first main role in *Rawhide* by killing off an image that had become a strait jacket. Rowdy Yates could now be shot down.[11]

External circumstances also played their part in sending Eastwood to Italy. At that time Hollywood was stuck in a state of inertia in which nothing new seemed to be happening. The studios seemed more and more resistant to change even as it was clear that the world was changing.[12] This stagnation was reflected by lower returns at the box office, reduced profits for the big studios and a reduction in the number of films being made. Even the artistic merit of the big studios' films seemed to be diminishing. With great masters of cinematography nowhere to be seen, Eastwood's training as an actor and director took place among others, through a form of indirect transmission. Leone, a huge fan of Hollywood cinema and also a former assistant director on many films by American directors shot in Italy, was to influence Eastwood. As did Don Siegel, the director who had previously been an editor and second-unit director working at Warner Bros. Studios as far back as the 1930s, on the films of Raoul Walsh, Michael Curtiz and Howard Hawks.

The Man with No Name

As opposed to the heavy atmosphere at Hollywood, Leone's cinematic works represented a fracture with the past and freedom, using fast, iconoclastic imagery and an almost childlike disregard for the grammar of classic film shots and accepted codes of morality. His westerns — and Eastwood's performances within them — revealed a near perfect synchronicity with the times, as their immediate and widespread success demonstrated. In step with the era but also prescient of an America to come, they foreshadowed a new Hollywood that was to devote much energy to portraying a new, violent, even explosive social reality. Pre-dating the 'new western' of the early 1970s, the Italian director's series of films pulled off a double feat, killing the genre in one sense but, in another, renewing it and ridding it forever of a need to strictly adhere to the established conventions of the genre. Leone created new horizons for the western, aesthetically and morally — and even in terms of

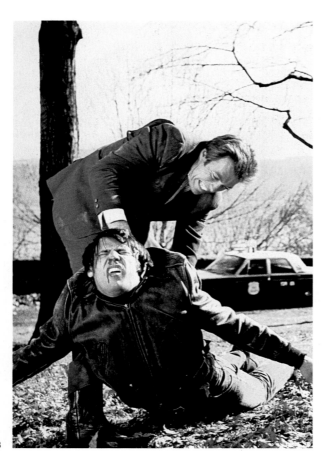

budget requirements. However, the press of the time immediately protested at the films' excess of violence and took offence at what they regarded as the Italian's impudent distortion of the western's sacrosanct form, accusing his films of being degenerate versions of the genre.[13]

The critics' discrediting of Leone's films was ultimately to affect Eastwood negatively, but on the other hand, he finally had a face. And what a face it was, unlike anyone else's at the time: fine-featured, even delicate, seductive but also disturbing, capable of tensing, even freezing into an implacable stare with the piercing, narrow eyes of a murderer. His concentrated expression created a focus in the scenes, which meant that sometimes he did not even have to do anything else in a shot; or, conversely, it proved the perfect filmic prelude for his character's lightning-quick responses, requiring no explanation. In short, his was the perfect 'action' face. Using an economy of means, it focused on maximizing effect and dispensing with psychological motivation, relying only on the power of the actor's presence. But one can look at Eastwood's wish to create an unusual image in another way. Eastwood wanted to prove his talent and originality as an actor and yet his decision to do the role backfired, as his image in the *Dollars* trilogy led critics to deem his acting style limited, even suggesting that he was just happy to be there.[14] Eastwood hadn't intended to make a career out of playing in Italian westerns but, once he had, critics and producers could not imagine him playing anything other than 'the man with the cigarillo'. Together, Leone and Eastwood had created this enigmatic character with no defined outline, cynical, even intriguing in his masochism. But, for Eastwood, playing gunfighters and bounty-hunters three times was more than enough. His character — according to many critics, sometimes indistinguishable from the actor himself — came over as contemptuous and macho: in short, beyond the pale.[15] It was this that led him to turn down a role in Leone's *Once Upon a Time in the West* (1968). Later, his desire to endlessly eliminate any clichés about his image was to be the motor behind his partnership with Don Siegel. Both strong characters, they were to make five films together, including, in 1968, *Coogan's Bluff* (a dry run for *Dirty Harry*, 1971) and *Escape from Alcatraz* (1979), one of their most accomplished films together.

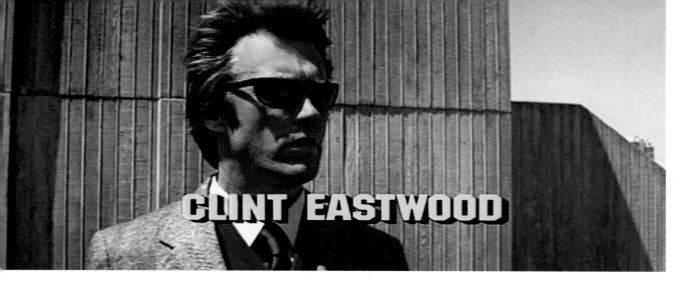

CLINT EASTWOOD

Opposite page: Clint Eastwood
and Don Stroud in Don Siegel's
Coogan's Bluff (1968).

Above: Clint Eastwood in
Don Siegel's *Dirty Harry* (1971).

The trouble with Harry

In May and June 1971, Siegel, Eastwood and the
talented cinematographer Bruce Surtees worked
together on a genre film for Warner Bros. entitled
Dirty Harry, which was to be released at Christmas
of the same year. The plot: a cop named Harry
Callahan, known as 'Dirty Harry', with a habit of
doing things his own way and a Magnum 44 at
his belt; a journey through San Francisco by day
and night; a serial killer who calls himself Scorpio;
a legal system that seems to care more about the
rights of criminals than those of the victims; and
a relentless hunt for a killer led by a progressively
more rebellious Callahan ready to use any means
necessary to achieve his ends. Summarized in this
way, it is clear how the film provided the critics
with a field day. This applied more particularly to
the American reviewers, who at that time regarded
all of Eastwood's films after his return to the U.S.
with condescension and contempt — at best, distrac-
tions without value and, at worst, a depressing new
sign of the times.[16]

And *Dirty Harry*'s crime? At the root of the
incomprehension it elicited — perhaps still elicits
— was its anti-authoritarian stance and expression of
a form of resistance, subversion and even rage that
did not fit into the counter-culture of the time. It
even seemed to pit itself against this counter-culture.
In short, its crime was to protest after its own fashion. Setting the libertarian impulse against the radical impulse (clearly Harry Callahan reflected Siegel
more than he realized), it invited an ideological
reading instead of a more nuanced critical analysis.

Clint Eastwood, by Pauline Kael

This was an unfair and inaccurate article, but an inevitable one, given the current rise of a counter-culture driven by artists who wanted to detach themselves from Nixon's repressive America. Needing to draw attention to their cause, they often ended up mimicking the very political and ideological intransigence they chose to condemn, dismissing works whose beauty and uniqueness became clear with the passing of time. This particular article by Pauline Kael – the dreaded New Yorker's film critic – created quite a stir when it was first published and for a long time afterwards. For over a decade it set the tone for the way Eastwood would be seen as an actor and filmmaker, turning him into the intelligentsia's very own bête noire and also prompting Eastwood to develop his own irrepressible inner critic. In short, this article was to have a crucial impact on his films and the future characters he would play, making it, paradoxically, essential reading.

Dirty Harry is not about the actual San Francisco police force; it's about a right-wing fantasy of that police force as a group helplessly emasculated by unrealistic liberals. The conceit of this movie is that for one brief, glorious period the police have a realist in their midst – and drive him out. [...] In the action genre, it's easier – and more fun – to treat crime in this medieval way, as evil, without specific causes or background. What produces a killer might be a subject for an artist, but it's a nuisance to an exciter, who doesn't want to slow the action down. You're making a picture with Clint Eastwood, you naturally want things to be simple, and the basic contest between good and evil is as simple as you can get. It makes this genre piece more archetypal than most movies, more primitive and dreamlike; fascist medievalism has a fairytale appeal.

The movie was cheered and applauded by Puerto Ricans in the audience, and they jeered – as they were meant to – when the maniac whined and pleaded for his legal rights. Puerto Ricans could applaud Harry because in the movie, laws protecting the rights of the accused are seen not as remedies for the mistreatment of the poor by the police and the courts but as protection for evil abstracted from all social conditions – metaphysical evil, classless criminality. The movie shrewdly makes the maniac smart, well-spoken, and white, and in order to clear Harry of any charge of prejudice or racism he is given a Mexican partner (Reni Santoni). The audience is led to identify totally with Harry and to feel victorious because the liberals don't succeed in stopping him. He saves us this time; he slaughters the maniac who has grabbed a busload of terrified children and is slapping them around. But Harry Callahan has to defy the mayor and the police department to do it. And, in a final gesture of contempt for the unrealistic legal system, Harry throws his badge into the same waters that the killer's corpse is floating in. Harry has dirtied himself for the last time; there is no one now to save us from evil, because the liberals are running the city. [...]

If you go along with the movie – and it's hard to resist, because the most skilful suspense techniques are used on very primitive emotional levels – you have but one desire: to see the maniac get it so it hurts. The movie lacks the zing and brute vitality of *The French Connection*; but it has such sustained drive toward this righteous conclusion that it is an almost perfect piece of propaganda for para-legal police power. The evil monster represents urban violence, and the audience gets to see him kicked and knifed and shot, and finally triumphantly drowned. Violence has rarely been presented with such righteous relish. [...]

On the way out, a pink-cheeked little girl was saying 'That was a good picture' to her father. Of course; the dragon had been slain. *Dirty Harry* is obviously just a genre movie, but this action genre has always had a fascist potential, and it has finally surfaced. If crime were caused by super-evil dragons, there would be no Miranda, no Escobedo; we could all be licensed to kill, like Dirty Harry. But since crime is caused by deprivation, misery, psychopathology, and social injustice, *Dirty Harry* is a deeply immoral movie.

This is an extract from the article 'Saint Cop', published in *The New Yorker*, 15 January 1972.

Opposite page and right:
Clint Eastwood in Don Siegel's
Dirty Harry (1971).

Above, top: Clint Eastwood in
Ted Post's *Magnum Force* (1973).

Above, bottom: Clint Eastwood in
James Fargo's *The Enforcer* (1976).

Opposite page: Clint Eastwood
and Bruce Dern in Ted Post's
Hang 'Em High (1968).

In an era when people were becoming more politicized in the United States, the film's own brand of radicalism and the general radical movement of the time were seen as completely incompatible and this in itself was enough for the critics to ignore some of the film's subtleties and ambiguities. As a result, *Dirty Harry* was unavoidably seen as a vehicle championing law and order and as some sort of mouthpiece for the views of President Nixon.

It was to be the highly influential *New Yorker* journalist Pauline Kael, self-proclaimed prophet-critic for the Woodstock generation and 'new' Hollywood, who would take criticism of Eastwood's films to a new level by attacking the film politically, accusing both the film and the main character Harry Callahan — and by implication Eastwood — of being racist and fascist. These accusations created a controversy around the film and also reverberated in people's minds throughout the years. For over a decade, at the very least, the actor was seen as a reactionary and, by the less generous-minded, as a Nazi. The accusations messed up Eastwood for a long time, to the point that he was to read out Kael's article to a psychoanalyst. And yet the film had tried to pre-empt these kinds of negative critical observations by taking certain precautions in its structure. In particular, the film clearly has two parts, which deliberately work to ensure the film's director and main character are not confused, as well as making a distinction between the character and the actor who plays him (Eastwood). It does this in the second part, where the story explores Callahan's character in more detail, rendering his dark side more explicit and foiling the more seductive spin put on his character in the first part. The film's dialectic of attraction and repulsion around the character Harry creates a kind of reverse catharsis during the course of the story, by destroying its own mythology and earlier presentation of Harry as a hero-type character. This happens right in the middle of the film, when it seems to suddenly turn, with an almost hallucinatory section capturing this pivotal point. Halfway through the nocturnal sequence, in a deserted Kezar Stadium in San Francisco, Harry is wounded, exhausted, his eyes bulging with excitement following his pursuit of Scorpio, whom he has managed to capture. In order to get the murderer to confess, Harry begins torturing him. At that exact moment, the camera (held aloft in a helicopter) pulls back physically and metaphorically from Harry, beginning an enormous backwards-travelling shot until the image literally fades as the men disappear out of sight, creating one of the most unusual shots of the film.[17] This tells us that more is at play than simply a progression from the films of Leone to those of Siegel. Eastwood is not just swapping a poncho for a Magnum, the countryside for the city, or playing sheriffs in New York. Compared to the Man with No Name, or Blondie in *The Good, The Bad and The Ugly* — characters that Leone deliberately presents as just surfaces, even simple cinematic silhouettes — Harry Callahan manifests depth and lives in a state of overwhelming anxiety. He is a loner, in the throes of grief and melancholic bitterness, which he tries to heal through action. He has the restlessness of an insomniac with no fixed abode, who spends his time on the street. In a scene that

foreshadows the behaviour of the character Travis Bickle in Martin Scorsese's *Taxi Driver* (1976), he lets loose a paranoid diatribe against the world. He is a man whose only sexual gratification seems to be the verbal and physical expression of violence and he has it in for the whole universe (and himself) because of the accidental death of his wife. He is a killing machine without any other human relationship. Above all, he takes pleasure from inflicting violence, and on some level, although he can't admit it to himself, he sees in the murderer Scorpio the terrifying image of a repressed person who has finally set himself free. Warner Bros. Studios dreamed up a tag line to launch the film, which they ultimately dropped, but which has since taken pride of place in Eastwood's office: 'Dirty Harry and the Homicidal Maniac. Harry's the one with the badge.' Is the badge the only thing that sets Harry apart from the murderer he hunts down?

Ripostes, replies and retouching

While Eastwood's celebrity was in the ascendant and he was arriving at a point where he could give expression to his artistic ambitions, the possibility of any kind of critical recognition seemed to correspondingly become more elusive. This contradictory state of affairs once again triggered his old desire to take control of his image, and the 1970s saw Eastwood graduate to directing his own films. The strength of this wish to control his image meant that, from *Dirty Harry* onwards, and even before the controversy around the release of that particular film, Eastwood was to systematically devote his creative energies as director and actor in developing films and characters, or perhaps more precisely, creating cinematic images of himself that critiqued the images constructed of him by the media and press. And if on some level he becomes the real subject of each of his films, this also reflects his greater power within the industry, as a result of setting up his own film company, Malpaso Productions, in 1967; and also because of his near-constant presence in the list of top ten most bankable stars in American cinema in the 1970s, topping the list three times during the decade (1972, 1973, 1979), ahead of John Wayne, Paul Newman and John Travolta.

In 1972 the issue was to be his political image. Seen as a reactionary, even as a fascist, he had not helped matters by admitting to voting Republican. And yet he also acted in Ted Post's 1968 film *Hang 'Em High*, a film whose liberalist slant looks at the impossibility of any kind of true vengeance, even the existentialist impasse of all personal justice, and also demonstrates a cold horror of state-sanctioned vengeance and capital punishment by hanging. However, because of the continuing legacy of *Dirty Harry*, Eastwood used the elegant *Magnum Force* (Ted Post, 1973) to try and set the record straight about the image others had of him.

First and foremost, the whole film can be seen as Eastwood's way of responding through a visual medium to the various accusations made in print about him. It would in fact not be unreasonable to say that it was one of those rare cases when actual criticism of the star, in the form of Pauline Kael's writings about him, actually engendered a screenplay. In summary, *Magnum Force*'s story is as follows: a motorbike squadron of traffic cops right at the heart of the San Francisco police department turn renegade and become judge and jury of whoever they see fit, executing people randomly. They try to enlist Harry Callahan, who they assume is like them. Crucially, he responds to them with, 'I'm afraid you have misjudged me' — as much the filmmaker's words to his detractors as the words of his character. Eastwood played with Kael's description of him by presenting the motorbike cops in leather and Ray-Bans, like some form of 'robot-portrait' of himself and a perfect surface upon which the audience could project its desires. By separating the character of Callahan from his darkest drives and

Above: Clint Eastwood and Shirley MacLaine in Don Siegel's *Two Mules for Sister Sara* (1970).

Right: Clint Eastwood and Sondra Locke in *The Gauntlet* (1977).

Following pages: Geraldine Page and Clint Eastwood in Don Siegel's *The Beguiled* (1971).

embodying these in the image of the 'fascist police motorcyclists', the film shrewdly creates a sense of distance and dissimilarity. This sets it apart from its predecessor, even if, as a result, Harry's personality loses some of its compelling neurotic madness along with the first film's indefinable atmosphere of ontological anxiety created by Siegel.

Clint on the cross

If *Magnum Force* sets up a particular paradigm, in fact all of Eastwood's films — albeit to a lesser extent — express a rage at not being properly understood or recognized. To the accusation — long present from the days of his work with Leone but now loaded with political criticism — that he was a male chauvinist and a misogynist, or a 'sado-macho', Eastwood was to respond on his own terms, using the *Dirty Harry* series as a means to an end. And so the third film in the series, *The Enforcer*, directed by James Fargo (1976) came along. Although a lazy film and a failure overall, it does have one aspect that brings a little life to it and creates some interest. This is Harry's relationship with his colleagues, in particular a female colleague, whose utter difference as a female when confronted with the brute aspect of Harry's character leads to his eventual humanization, albeit represented in a rather forced way. Paradoxically, this is also what makes this particular story about America's favourite cop a little dull. However, this was certainly not the first time Eastwood had decided to experiment with his image in relation to the 'weaker sex', often giving a female actor the 'better' role in a film,[18] which of course was to trigger off an avalanche of criticism and polemic about his patronizing sexism during this era, from a critical community seemingly incapable of believing that Eastwood possessed any kind of sincerity.

The most striking aspect of Eastwood's films of this period is actually the opposite of the sadism of which they are generally accused: it is his characters' overwhelming masochism that is remarkable. The list of physical abuses they suffer is endless.[19] It seems they follow a cinematic code that had been in place since the 1950s and Anthony Mann's five westerns with James Stewart: all heroes are suffering heroes. In fact, they must enjoy it all the more in order to enhance their heroic status. Eastwood often presents the audience with an ecstasy of expiation in his films — even his character

in the implausible *Every Which Way But Loose* (1978) admits to enjoying being hit. Few actors have taken the destruction of their image so far and so literally. And no other actor has played roles or directed films with characters who begin their stories with such a surfeit of cynicism and pleasure in their own erotic power (*The Beguiled*, 1971; *Play Misty for Me*, 1971), or who are selfish, arrogantly aloof or misanthropic (William Holden in *Breezy*, 1973), or self-important and élitist (*The Eiger Sanction*, 1975). All these films set up caricatures that Eastwood seems to wilfully dismantle during the course of the narrative, in order to be free of them.

Just an image but the right image

As a fitting summation of their decade of work, *Escape from Alcatraz* (1979) was the last film Eastwood and Siegel made together, and also Siegel's third from final work. The entire film focuses on the meticulous preparation made by Frank Morris (Eastwood) for an escape from the infamous prison located in the environs of San Francisco, from which they say nobody has ever escaped. In order to trick the prison guards, Morris builds a model of his face made from soaked paper. Here again we have a *trompe-l'oeil* and a false face long-believed by the guards to be the character's real one. When a guard finally discovers the hoax, the mask falls to the floor, but the feat of deception has been pulled off: Morris is free. And one could say at this point, so is Eastwood.

Above: Kay Lenz and William Holden in *Breezy* (1973).

Below: Clint Eastwood in Don Siegel's *Escape from Alcatraz* (1979).

Opposite page: *The Gauntlet* (1977).

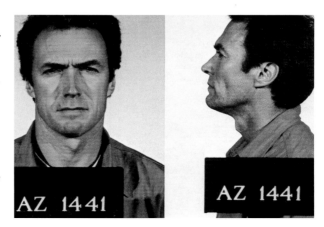

28

At point-blank range
The Gauntlet

In this curiosity of a film, half-way between a road movie and a comedy about the war between the sexes, a cop who is a bit slow on the uptake and a quick-witted prostitute are tracked throughout, like some kind of moving target, by a group of militia-like police. Twenty minutes into the film, the man and the woman – Detective Shockley (Eastwood) and Gus (Sondra Locke) – think they can hide in Gus's lair, a low and wide house on a roadside in the middle of nowhere. However, an armed-to-the teeth phalanx of cops descends and encircles the house, turning their refuge into an ambush. A sustained attack on the house begins as the forces of 'order' open fire and rain down rifle shots on the house, matched by a dizzying sequence of film shots. From the moment the cops first open fire to the last groan of the house as it collapses, seventy separate shots occur in less than two and a half minutes. Why this frenzied run of images?

Eastwood explained where he got the idea for the sequence. He had seen images of the SLA (Symbionese Liberation Army) house being destroyed, live on TV on 17 May 1974, and had been particularly struck by the form the assault took on this small group of left-wing militants. 'Over five hundred LAPD police (Los Angeles Police Department) and FBI agents shot 9,000 times at their house before setting it ablaze… it was a conflagration created by tragedy and farce in equal amounts' (David E. James, *Cinéma 012*, 2006). In other words, the most extreme fictional scenarios of the time were only copying a world gone crazy – the terrorists and liberation militias of the 1970s. His explanation also underlines how all fiction is merely a way of documenting reality and so, in a sense, is a form of documentary itself. It would also seem that the film had a far more biographical source and can be

read as a kind of hallucinogenic commentary on Eastwood's private life, which resembled a battlefield at the time. Eastwood was in the process of building a Hollywood-style residence at Pebble Beach called Forever House, which would become a true architectural folly and would take seven years to complete. (A seven-year itch?) His affair with Sondra Locke had become more serious and his marriage was at risk of collapsing. In the film, Shockley is holed up in a house, under fire, and trying to

avoid the sky falling in on him in a hail of shots. Crucially, he manages to slip away and join his fugitive beauty. Another example of Eastwood's game of cinematic masochism? Here it is taken to a point of absolute extremity and also leads to a point of rupture, an agonizing struggle and then ideal resolution. The filmmaker and his first wife were to separate in 1979, before officially divorcing in 1984.

The film's main motif of a man under siege, shot at from all sides and unable to defend

himself, who eventually escapes through the cellar, can also be read as Eastwood's way of once and for all disarming his Dirty Harry character for his viewers. It highlights Eastwood's need at the time to liberate himself from and transcend any image already held about him. The furious energy of this sequence and its endless gunfire can be seen as a visual and sonic representation of an over-the-top and caricatured masculinity that Eastwood ultimately 'escapes' in the film.

Finding Community

From *The Outlaw Josey Wales* to *Pale Rider*

Clint Eastwood in *The Outlaw Josey Wales* (1976).

Right: Clint Eastwood and Don Rickles in Brian G. Hutton's *Kelly's Heroes* (1970).

By the middle of the 1970s, Eastwood had already acquired a wealth of knowledge about the art of directing films (and also the role of producer), through the school of hard knocks, perhaps. But, as somebody who had always wanted to learn as much as possible by any means, he had retained all that he had learned from his array of very different experiences, which now proved invaluable in his graduation to filmmaker.

Eastwood's experience on the catastrophic shoot of Jodie Copeland's *Ambush at Cimarron Pass* (1958) as a young actor fresh out of Universal's 'stables' had showed him first-hand how a film could nosedive artistically as a result of lack of preparation, means and vision. During the endless filming of *Rawhide* he learned the fundamentals of directing by heart, and with Leone, the art of heightening and magnifying a film's on-screen effect, masterfully demonstrated in *A Fistful of Dollars*. Even as he was sharing top billing as star on Joshua Logan's *Paint Your Wagon* (1969), an old-school Hollywood musical comedy, he never forgot witnessing how the production poured away millions of dollars as a result of a time-wasting shoot that never seemed to end and yet produced meagre results. All this led to him promising himself at the time that if ever he got the chance to direct, he would ensure his film would stay within budget and come in on schedule. After filming, in Yugoslavia, the lavishly produced *Kelly's Heroes* (1970), directed by Brian Hutton, Eastwood also observed how a director could lose control of his film to the studio during the editing stage. He had also observed Vittorio De Sica making his segment of *Le streghe* (*The Witches*, 1967). Finally, and most importantly, he learnt from Siegel at the outset of their partnership what would become his own personal filmmaking credo: everything possible should be done to try and make the first take the best and to be able to recognize when you have got it right, in order to capture the spontaneity in an actor's performance — not to mention the money and time saved as a result. He had also by this time already made a short documentary about Siegel during the making of *The Beguiled*, and had directed the suicide rescue sequence in *Dirty Harry*. Inversely, he was to give a small role to his mentor in his own film, *Play Misty for Me*, the first for him as a director. While *Play Misty for Me* is clearly influenced by *The Beguiled*, it also reveals the beginnings of Eastwood's more sentimental side. His film *Breezy* (1973) developed this romantic aspect, while his first western, *High Plains Drifter*

(1973), conversely applied a harsh style influenced by Leone. During the same period he also made what is ultimately a strange and rather unsatisfactory spy film, *The Eiger Sanction*, set against the natural backdrop of a Swiss alpine landscape and the dominating peak of the Eiger, which seems to take a starring role in the film.

During the shoot of *The Outlaw Josey Wales*, at the end of 1975, Eastwood already had four films under his belt as director. Yet, in some senses *Josey Wales* should really be regarded as his real directorial début. It is with this film's definitive success and artistic accomplishment that Eastwood found his feet and confirmed any unresolved questions about his future ability as a genuine filmmaker.

Crossing over, taking the plunge

Right from his early success as an actor in the United States and then with his later work with Siegel, Eastwood had never been fully satisfied with the way Universal Studios had promoted his work.[20] The studio's publicity campaign for *The Beguiled*, hardly a typical film by any standards, proved too conventional for Eastwood and in 1975, between Universal's release of *The Eiger Sanction* and the

Below: *The Outlaw Josey Wales* (1976).

Opposite page: Sondra Locke in *The Outlaw Josey Wales* (1976).

Following pages: Will Sampson and Clint Eastwood in *The Outlaw Josey Wales* (1976).

beginning of the filming of *Josey Wales*, Eastwood decided to definitively jump ship and change studio, moving his production company Malpaso to the Warner buildings.

Having gained a lot from their absorption into the Kinney National Company in 1969, Warner Bros. had been presided over by the former Hollywood talent agent Ted Ashley from that time and crucially had the elegant and efficient John Calley at its helm as head of production, backed up by Frank Wells as his second in command, in charge of the studio's finances. (Wells was also, incidentally, Eastwood's lawyer.) Joe Hyams completed the talented ensemble by heading up its publicity department. As a result, Warner Bros. proved a force to be reckoned with during the 1970s, supporting and introducing new talent into the American film business (including William Friedkin's *The Exorcist* and Martin Scorsese's *Mean Streets*, both in 1973) and also championing an *auteur*-based system of filmmaking that accorded directors the role of executive producer on their productions and allowed them the final cut of their films.[21]

Clearly this new approach and environment played a definitive role in the success of *Josey Wales*,

which heralded a fruitful partnership between Warner Bros. and Eastwood that endures to this day. The film benefited from and also marked the beginnings of other important encounters for Eastwood, in particular his meeting with Sondra Locke, who would go on to be his personal partner for thirteen years and would also act with him in seven of his films. More than this, *Josey Wales* marked Eastwood's coming out as a director. In fact, Eastwood fired the film's original director and scriptwriter Philip Kaufman after just fifteen days of shooting, taking his place and securing his absolute authority over the film. Although he received fines and reprimands from the Directors Guild of America as a result, his action clearly demonstrated his belief in his own artistic vision and an irrepressible desire to express himself as a filmmaker, even using this new role to assure his freedom as an actor. It is precisely with *Josey Wales* that Eastwood finally gains control over his image and his concept of character. In fact, from here on in, every film in which Eastwood acted was to also have him in the director's seat. And later on, if the credits of certain films list another as director — for example, James Fargo, Richard Tuggle, Richard Benjamin or Buddy Van

Horn (whose careers as directors were promoted by Eastwood) or even credits the name of an established professional like Wolfgang Petersen, the director of *In the Line of Fire* (1993), who was not part of the Malpaso 'stable' — one thing remains constant: if Eastwood is acting in a film, he ultimately runs the creative show.[22]

In *Josey Wales*, Eastwood's character has an inner violence that cannot be exhausted by any outward violent action, but during the course of his journey he becomes the ringleader of a group of disparate characters brought together by fate, who in return lead him to a form of inner peace, as long he is able to be in charge. In a sense, this character is a reflection and sublimation of Eastwood the person and filmmaker, who would similarly show himself able to take on the collective experience, making it one of his most important cinematic subjects. Between the years 1976 and 1985, the filmmaker was to gather around him and organize various different communities, in his films as in his life.

Towards a cinematic destiny

Converging many strands of his career artistically and professionally, the western *The Outlaw Josey Wales* required Eastwood to explore his own cinematic influences and modes of storytelling. After Leone and his game of massacre, what could one add? Indeed what could one do that went beyond the graphically staged pessimism of Siegel's works? Clearly, for both filmmakers, their films were not simply about cynicism or nihilism. Leone's films expressed the idealist's disappointment and Siegel's films were an almost prescient display of man's progressive inhumanity. And equally, their characters were always individualists, if only as a result of circumstance. As the 1970s reached their mid-point, the question seemed to be what kind of fiction could one create to bring closure to the events of Vietnam, which had officially ended but which had left in its wake millions of dead on both sides, shell-shocked survivors and an America now at war with itself? How could one believe in a system stripped bare by the Watergate scandal, which had forced Nixon to resign and had created a crisis about representative leadership? After so much destruction, deconstruction, distortion and collapse, Eastwood's western seems to take the only path left at that time — that of rebirth and reconstitution. Using the stories of

Did you say westerns?

Yes: more than two hundred episodes of *Rawhide*, Sergio Leone's historical trilogy, *Hang 'Em High*, *Two Mules for Sister Sara*, *Joe Kidd* (to a lesser extent), two films that are unclassifiable (*The Beguiled*, *Bronco Billy*) and, of course, *High Plains Drifter*, *The Outlaw Josey Wales*, *Pale Rider* and *Unforgiven*. Having made it late both on screen and behind the camera within the genre (some might say the last of its great figures), Eastwood still managed to leave an indelible mark on this singularly American invention, which, continuing the tradition of Homer, creates an epic of America's Wild West. He devised his own new blueprint for the genre, as well as bringing its themes full circle to cover new ground and directions.

Eastwood's *Josey Wales*, released in 1976, was already bringing up the rear of a highly criticized and disenchanted form of western made in the early 1970s (including Sam Peckinpah's *The Wild Bunch* as early 1969 and Arthur Penn's *Little Big Man* of 1970). Called 'Vietnam westerns', they indirectly explored America's aggression in Southeast Asia and rewrote American history and the rules of the genre. As a result, the flow of westerns ground to a halt after 1976 and, except for the sublime *Heaven's Gate* (Michael Cimino, 1980), it barely survived – apart from Eastwood's westerns, which would appear every ten years and the last of which, *Unforgiven* (1992), was to masterfully strip to the core America's founding myths about its conquering race.

Even more so in relation to each other, Eastwood's westerns seem to have an ongoing dialogue, each new one in the series suggesting a response to an earlier offering. *Pale Rider* seems to take up the motifs of *High Plains Drifter* (a unknown man who appears on the horizon and ultimately returns to it), while also inverting its themes (the essence of cowardice/the birth of courage), and *Unforgiven*, his most recent contribution, contains and summarizes all his earlier forays into the genre. Not only do Eastwood's westerns have a finality – a way of closing the door behind them before setting back off into the horizon, returning to the eternity and nothingness of the final shot of John Wayne in *The Searchers* (John Ford, 1956) – they also present a review of some of the genre's most important and iconic works of an earlier era. *High Plains Drifter* radicalizes and mocks *High Noon* (Fred Zinnemann, 1952) and pays a last tribute to Leone's ironic approach to the genre, while *Josey Wales* refers to and draws inspiration from at least three earlier important works: *Yellow Sky* (William Wellman, 1948), *Run of the Arrow* (Samuel Fuller, 1957) and, as already mentioned, *The Searchers*. These earlier films all exhibit a similar anxiety around the need to establish a sense of elusive community, as well as introducing a central character who is full of rage and resistant to the laws of the conquerors and the progress of civilization. One can say that *Pale Rider* evokes *Shane* (George Stevens, 1953) and *Unforgiven*, although seemingly taking up the themes of *Man of the West* (Anthony Mann, 1958) in its study of a former murderer forced to take up the bloodshed of his past again. *Unforgiven* also reversed John Ford's famous axiom 'When the legend becomes fact, print the legend', continuing the demystification project already present in Ford's *The Man Who Shot Liberty Valance* (1962), which was prompted by the political necessity of disrupting a persistent set of western imagery in films whose power was able to pass off various fictions as historical truths.

Ultimately, Eastwood's westerns conclude the genre's place in history but also the history of the genre itself. They have this sense of dual justification but are also tempered and counterpointed by Eastwood's inimitable on-screen presence, the scale of his body and particular face simultaneously evoking a memory of the origins and earlier archetypal characters. Eastwood's cinematic presence recalls another large body and unique face, that of William S. Hart (1864–1946), one of cinema's first true cowboys, a handsome hero of the silent era, known at the time as 'The man from nowhere' and 'The man with the light eyes'. He too was an elegant actor and filmmaker, and seems an earlier form of Eastwood's characters, an older brother even:

'No one ever knows where he comes from. He passes through, roaming the West and its great vastness. He arrives on horseback, comes down off his horse into the land of men. The time he spends in the company of men is a time of suffering, meaning it is a time he spends trying to love others. When his brow has been sufficiently furrowed and he has shaken his fists enough… he refuses to continue suffering on the land or the confines of a room and he gets back up on his horse and that's it, he's gone… I think we have cinema here.'
(Louis Delluc, February 1919.)

Opposite page: Clint Eastwood in
Unforgiven (1992).

Above: *The Outlaw Josey Wales* (1976).

cinema and the state of the world to suggest a new kind of humanism, this centres on the idea of a man that abandons no one at the roadside and restores the threads of humanity and lines of narrative by taking up the continuity of the western genre's founding myths, through a rereading and re-examination of them.

A survivor who has witnessed the massacre of his whole family during the horrors of America's Civil War, the character Josey Wales goes off to fight in order to rid himself of hate, in a vain attempt to dispel his rage by going deep into his own violence and, he hopes, dying in the process.[23] Initially a member of a small community of Confederate soldiers, all the men in the community are united by a form of pure negativity (a community of disenfranchised men, a community of the dead). Once the war has finished — apart from the one within him — Wales takes off on a long journey that sees him develop a new power of attraction like some preacher of the unconscious, who works through silence. Wales gathers around him a group of people adrift, the survivors of disaster, what is left of America after the *tabula rasa* of war (the Civil War, the Vietnam War). He meets a little boy who dies

en route, an irresistible old Indian chief, a squaw called Moonlight, an abandoned dog, an irascible grandmother and her strange daughter-in-law, the last few dwellers of a ghost town and, finally, Ten Bears, the Comanche chief.[24] A community born out of ashes and grief, they represent a smaller personal community that becomes like an extended family of individuals. The film seems to contain political implications about how people should live together, with a strong accent on rural life. Wales seems to be a syncretic figure, part Viet Cong guerrilla and part Founding Father, and a dead man reborn into life. Eastwood found the character he wanted to be, as well as using the film to make a commentary on the United States of the time. He finds a personal subject here, the dream of a community embodying reconciliation, a dream whose nightmare side he had already explored in *High Plains Drifter*. Later, in *Pale Rider*, he was to go as far as creating a sequence that literally embodied his mythical vision of the 'Birth of a Nation'. In the scenes around the campfire, Surtees, Eastwood's cinematographer, seems to re-create the subject matter of the famous Rembrandt painting, *The Night Watch*: a group of men together at night, talking and sharing their thoughts, decides to resist tyranny. In *Pale Rider* the men are individuals who have nothing, poor gold-panning miners at risk of being pushed out of their mining community, but they decide to fight back. In short, it portrays how political will and the spirit of democracy are born.

Perhaps it was no coincidence that, in January 1986, Eastwood announced that he would run for mayor in the town where he lived (Carmel, Northern California), a community that had certainly enjoyed peace for a long time. Elected in April with 2,166 votes (72.5 per cent of the count), his term of office was to last for two years.

The dream of community

If Eastwood's taste for community does not really come into play in *Firefox*, a film more about paranoid tension within and between groups (in this case, the United States and the USSR), it is not typical of Eastwood's films at this time, which generally tend towards presenting free, rebellious or libertarian communities. Even the family in *Every Which Way But Loose* reflects this, and its rather more rushed follow-up, *Any Which Way You Can* (1980), also offers up a community of sorts: two inseparable

friends, a rather disgraceful old lady, a female country-music singer who can be a bitch when she feels like it, a jolly female hitchhiker picked up on the way and, of course, Clyde, the very laid-back orangutan. Even a particularly stupid band of Hells Angels, 'The Black Widows', is part of this strange tableau of characters.[25]

In this vein of happy communities, it is worth mentioning the warmth and hospitality of the dives, dancehalls and brothels of *Honkytonk Man*, but it is another film, *Bronco Billy* (1980), which explores the same themes as *Josey Wales* in a very different way, using the form of a fable, that reveals Eastwood's often anachronistic vision. In this work, an idea of the West is suggested, this time in a contemporary setting as the filmmaker 're-represents a perfect world' according to his own terms. The film's eponymous character, whose has given himself the same initials as Buffalo Bill, seems to live in total denial of his present reality, a kind of innocent that only madmen and children understand. He is a John Doe, the anonymous man of the street (also used by Frank Capra in his *Meet John Doe*, 1941), who has seemingly reincarnated as a 'real' cowboy now living in a cynical and materialistic contemporary

Opposite page: Billy Curtis and Clint Eastwood in *High Plains Drifter* (1973).

Above, top: Clint Eastwood and William Smith in Buddy Van Horn's *Any Which Way You Can* (1980).

Above, bottom: Clint Eastwood and Clyde in James Fargo's *Every Which Way But Loose* (1978).

Following pages: Clint Eastwood in *Bronco Billy* (1980).

America, very often paying dear for the character he has invented for himself because the harshness of reality impinges on his vision.

Again, the theme of community: Bronco Billy needs to share his dream with others — with the spectators of his Wild West show and also with his little troupe of beaten-up no-hopers. These include, among others, the squaw Running Water and her clumsy oaf of a husband, chief Big Eagle, a black ringmaster and, of course, 'the best lassoer in the West' as well as an elderly 'human canon', now banned from working because of ill health. At the beginning of *Josey Wales* we see a family house burning down and an atrocity: a wife and child murdered. In short, we are confronted with images of war. At the end of *Bronco Billy*, the show's big top also burns and in order that the show can go on another one is made using a hundred U.S. flags sewn together. We might well be observing old-fashioned patriotism here but, as always with Eastwood, there is another meaning at play. This is the patchwork quilt America has become after the experience of the Vietnam War, or that it had always been but refused to see in itself: a nation made up of many different people from all over the world, a country of different ethnicities, minorities, immigrants and 'pariahs'. With *Bronco Billy*, Eastwood once again re-enchants American history by demystifying it. He makes it a living history, a story for America's future as much as a reflection of its present, re-working American narratives about its past by re-writing them, opening them up and using them to recognize the differences between people as opposed to their similarities: Native Americans, African-Americans, Chinese, Irish, Mexicans and Latinos. We are introduced to each of them, one by one, in a way any filmmaker would do when presenting 'characters' in a film.

Eastwood will do the same in his presentation of the inhabitants of the small town of Savannah (Georgia) in a much later and enjoyable film, *Midnight in the Garden of Good and Evil* (1997). In fact, it is worth asking what the community of individuals he gives us in this film is if not some kind of strange vision of the ideal community? It is a perfect world where the living and dead exist together, where oddity and whim are allowed to cohabit: a man who walks an invisible dog, a man who keeps pet horse-flies, and a voodoo priestess, Lady

Chablis, who plays herself in the film and presides over her realm like an elemental fiery queen. A black transsexual, Lady Chablis ultimately embodies Eastwood's ideal, in the way she fuses masculine and feminine, and represents the harmonious cohabitation of difference, a community within. Similarly, in *Blood Work* (2002) Eastwood proffers his body on screen as a social space, a 'social body' where two selves meet. His character is given a heart transplant using the organ from a deceased Mexican woman. Eastwood was to also confide to a journalist after the release of *Bird* in 1988, that he had always felt like 'a black man in a white man's body'. Eastwood or the American Dream?

The music of the spheres

As well as the more sombre side to which he gives expression in his films, there is also a Bronco Billy inside Eastwood: a simple man dreaming of a happy concord between souls, and like Franklin D. Roosevelt when he spoke about America's forgotten men during his formulation of the New Deal in the Depression years, Eastwood addresses those left behind by society. This sensitive attention to the living, to life in all its forms, extends logically to all of nature's communities, human and animal. The sum of his works offers a vast bestiary of creatures as well as a reference to a kind of new 'ark'.[26] Eastwood's ark?

This communion with nature and an intuitive relationship with the world belong to a significant American tradition that predates Eastwood. Its origins lie in transcendentalism, a philosophical and literary movement of the first part of the nineteenth century, whose exponents include Henry David Thoreau (*Walden; or, Life in the Woods*) and Walt Whitman (*Leaves of Grass*). The movement originally inspired various utopian communes, including the Brook Farm experiment (near Boston, Massachusetts, 1841—7), seemingly evoked in the vision of the Blood Butte ranch in *Josey Wales*. Eastwood also privileges autumnal light in his westerns and each of his films demonstrates a subtle knowledge of the geography and aspects of each of America's different states, as revealed in the film *Thunderbolt and Lightfoot* (1974), starring Eastwood and directed by Michael Cimino, whose work masterfully captured the vastness of the American landscape (*Heaven's Gate*, 1980). Eastwood also allows for an ecological perspective in *Pale Rider* (the early capitalists of the

42

Below: Marty Robbins (left) and Clint Eastwood in *Honkytonk Man* (1982).

Opposite page, top: John McIntire, Clint Eastwood and Kyle Eastwood in *Honkytonk Man* (1982).

Opposite page, bottom: Kyle Eastwood (right) in *Honkytonk Man* (1982).

Gold Rush and their destruction of the land and forests through the use of high-pressure water jets in hydraulic mining). Above all, he reverses the usual privileging of man's dominion in the relationship between man and nature, making it clear that it is a false dominion, and focuses instead on the totemic majesty of the elements and the mountains, whose presence open and close *Pale Rider* and also figure in *The Eiger Sanction*, where the Eiger's unconquered peak is the film's final image.

This focus on the landscape probably explains, in part, one of Eastwood's stylistic signatures, an irrepressible enthusiasm for nature that often leads him to open and close a film with a panoramic shot of the landscape, filmed from a helicopter, which works to restore the vastness of nature to the centre of the story and establish the real dimensions of space; this also places man within a vast environment, which establishes relativity and the true scale of things before focusing in on a particular location or a house. From this perspective it is possible to see

43

music in Eastwood's works — jazz, country music, or the tribute paid to the songs of Johnny Mercer on the soundtrack of *Midnight in the Garden of Good and Evil* — as a particular kind of filmic 'space'. Because, what is popular song — for example, Snuff Garrett's ballads (in *Bronco Billy* or *Honkytonk Man*) — if not quite literally 'a common space', a space that all can share, a common language and an anti-Babel, as well as an experience of unity 'during which the rhythmic pulsation of a composition becomes our own'?[27] It is a reinvented space that takes on the status of a utopia, or even better, a 'heterotopia' — to borrow Michel Foucault's term elaborated in his essay 'Des espaces autres'.[28]

A heterotopia: an 'other' place, a different social space, a utopia which is not just an idea but also a place in the world. For example, the evening in the Oakland Civic Auditorium in 1946 when the young Eastwood heard Charlie Parker play for the first time, or a scene of triumphal performance in Paris, re-created by Eastwood as a rectangle of light, the filmic space in which Parker plays during a scene from *Bird*, and, again, the music studio that records the songs of the 'honkytonk' man. A heterotopia can also be any of the following: a pink Cadillac, a bullet-proof bus, a stolen Ford car, a space shuttle, a barricaded house, or a museum, a farm, Africa, a wooden house in California, a group of random people, a platoon of Marines, the earth seen from the sky, a campfire, the town of Savannah or *Bronco Billy*'s big top — in other words, 'a space of illusion that exposes real spaces as even more illusory' (Foucault).

A *common* space

As if in tandem with Eastwood's cinematic vision conclusively taking shape, refining and expressing

Clint Eastwood and Geoffrey
Lewis in Michael Cimino's
Thunderbolt and Lightfoot (1974).

Below: Clint Eastwood at Cannes
Film Festival in 1985.

itself (as well as confirming Eastwood's mastery
of both film and himself), two real communities were also crystallizing around the filmmaker
between 1976 and 1985, groups that endure to this
day. One was an intentional band of people brought
together under the auspices of his production company Malpaso; the other, a more dispersed community of people in France and America, who began to
do what would have been unimaginable a decade
earlier — generate critical support for Eastwood's
work and eventually set in motion a spectacular
ideological and critical U-turn on the part of the
critics about his films.

Originally small and set up as a structure to
help Eastwood develop more contacts and clout in
the films he was working on or developing, Malpaso
had evolved over the years into something far more
interesting. From around the time he began to work
on his own personal projects such as *The Beguiled*
and *Play Misty for Me*, reassured by his box-office
success in the 1970s[29] and support from a major
studio,[30] Eastwood's production company started
to turn into a genuine creative hub, like a jazz
ensemble or quintet. In fact, it too became a heterotopia, a space in which all manner of things
could arise. In all this, Eastwood is the 'ensemble leader', taking his 'instrumentalists' from film
to film,[31] promoting some from one film to the

next,[32] in a continuous line to this day. Loosely led by Eastwood, everyone does their thing, but the focus is on the overall ensemble and the creation of 'compositions' together, i.e. preparing the lighting, design and sound for current or future projects. Thanks to the Malpaso team, Eastwood has also used, even developed, a method he first learnt with Siegel, which focuses and serves the actor and creates a welcoming and supportive environment in which they can work.

Critical voices and *vox populi*

As people have slowly begun to pick up on Eastwood's way of working communally, a second community, of critical supporters, has developed around him, all the more remarkable because there were times when it seemed as though this could never happen.

In the beginning, signs of critical support were few and far between in America, as Pauline Kael and her successors maintained a central position in directing critical thinking about the filmmaker, whose work they held in open contempt. But in France, after the initial strong reaction towards *Dirty Harry* and, coming in its wake, *High Plains Drifter*, described by the magazine *Positif*, in January 1974, as 'a *Mein Kampf* of the Wild West', one sees signs of a softening towards Eastwood in some of the shorter pieces in the same magazine during 1975 and also in *Cahiers du cinéma* a little later.[33] Finally, on 10 December 1980, the prestigious Museum of Modern Art in New York took the initiative by programming *A Day with Clint Eastwood*, which screened four of the director's films in his presence. He was to remember it as one of the happiest days of his life. Next, the writer Norman Mailer wrote in defence of *Honkytonk Man* and resisted the critical establishment a year later by following this up with a flattering portrait of Eastwood, the man and filmmaker, in the Sunday press. Finally, it was to be the turn of Orson Welles …

One wonders whether Welles, like Wales (Josey), had the fictional hero's outlaw and maverick tendencies — as well as having a similar name. Or maybe Eastwood and Welles had a common enemy in Kael. However, it was not until 1982 that the maker of *Citizen Kane* unexpectedly appeared on American TV publically praising *The Outlaw Josey Wales* as well as decreeing that Eastwood was 'the most under-estimated director in the world'. People took note. In

August 1984, *Tightrope* (with Richard Tuggle credited as director) opened the Montréal World Film Festival, while, in France, Jean-Luc Godard dedicated his *Détective* (1985) to John Cassavetes, Edgar G. Ulmer and Clint Eastwood (three independent filmmakers?). As if in a return gesture, in *Heartbreak Ridge* (1986) the Eastwood character looks like Ferdinand at the end of *Pierrot le fou* (1965). Finally, from 19 December 1984 to 14 January 1985, Paris's Cinémathèque française (the French national film archive) showed Eastwood's works, both as director and actor, in their entirety, including even some of his *Rawhide* episodes. From this point onwards

Pale Rider (1985).

there were further retrospectives and, for the first time, an Eastwood film, *Pale Rider*, entered into competition at the Cannes Film Festival. This film was also to trigger a deluge of positive articles in the United States and even prompted the critical 'conversion' of *The New York Times* critic Vincent Canby.[34] France honoured Eastwood with an Ordre des Arts et Lettres and he also received a Cecil B. DeMille Award (for lifetime achievement) at the Golden Globes in January 1988. This all added up to a critical recognition that was to reach a first peak with his film *Bird*, followed by *Unforgiven*'s nine nominations and four Oscars in March 1993.

Clint Eastwood discusses his method

I haven't worked with a lot of big-name directors, but I came up during an era when they were all beginning to retire: I never worked with Hitchcock or Wyler or Stevens or Capra or Hawks or Walsh. I missed all that.

I suppose the most expensive director I've worked with is Don Siegel. I think I learned more about directing from him than from anybody else. He taught me to put myself on the line. He shoots lean, and he shoots what he wants. He knew when he had it, and he didn't need to cover his ass with a dozen different angles.

I learned that you have to trust your instincts. There's a moment when an actor has it, and he knows it. Behind the camera you can feel that moment even more clearly. And once you've got it, once you feel it, you can't second-guess yourself. If I would go around and ask everyone on the set how it looked, eventually someone would say, 'Well, gee, I don't know, there was a fly 600 feet back.' Somebody's always going to find a flaw, and pretty soon that flaw gets magnified and you're all back to another take. Meanwhile, everyone's forgotten that there's a certain focus on things, and no one's going to see that fly, because you're using a 100mm lens. But that's what you can do. You can talk yourself in or out of anything. You can find a million reasons why something didn't work. But if it feels right, and it looks right, it works. [...]

The critics are beginning to say that you've made some pretty good choices. Some of them. But it's luck. It's instinctive. It comes from the animal part of the brain: the instinctive, intuitive part. The analytical brain can kill you as an artist. You want to stay in touch on a deeper level.

This is an extract from Tim Cahill, 'Clint Eastwood', *Rolling Stone*, 4 July 1985 (reprinted in Robert E. Kapsis and Kathie Coblentz [eds], *Clint Eastwood: Interviews*, University Press of Mississippi, 1999).

Opposite page: Clint Eastwood in *Pale Rider* (1985).

Right: Don Siegel, Jessica Walter and Clint Eastwood on the set of *Play Misty for Me* (1971).

When night falls

In 1985, Eastwood directed the film *Pale Rider*, a noir western. Like the character of Josey Wales nearly ten years earlier, and in fact even more so than the earlier hero, the Pale Rider takes on the responsibility for a community. Also due to him, men, women and children gather together. And yet, as if he is merely a physical embodiment of an idea or its development, at the end the pale knight seems to fade back into the natural landscape, just as he seemed to have emerged out of it at the beginning. Like an 'undead' spirit who can never die, Josey Wales seems to have returned, briefly taking human form once again in order to create a new family and community, but as a wandering spirit, who can never expire, he cannot stay. In ten years, what darkness had obscured the journey towards the light, the theme of Eastwood's earlier film? Would there finally be a community for all, except for our roaming hero? Would there still be a happy ending?

A discussion about method: a dark light

Joel Cox (editor). It's not important if an actor forgets part of the script, or if he uses one word instead of another. What he [Eastwood] looks for is the truth in the scene. This is why he likes natural light so much. Correct me if I am wrong, Tom, but he hates having an over-lit image [...] If we were filming in this room now using the natural shadows the light is casting on our faces or on the different elements in the scene, he would rather work within these constraints. Certain cinematographers want to light everything so you can see it all. But Eastwood really doesn't want to see everything.

Tom Stern (cinematographer, previously a gaffer on Eastwood's films). I remember filming *Pale Rider*. We were in Seattle and there was a Van Gogh exhibition on there. I took a print of Van Gogh's work *The Potato Eaters* onto the set and I showed it to Bruce Surtees [Eastwood's cinematographer] and Clint, suggesting we shoot very under-exposed interiors and also add extra light to the exteriors. We discussed it and Clint agreed to shoot the images in this way, taking the contrast between the two as far as it could go. Clint had enough trust in Bruce to play in absolute darkness, to the point we could only see his face right at the end of the dialogue. I used to love what he would say to me when we were filming this kind of scene: 'Listen, at this point, we've already got through six reels worth of the story. If people haven't recognized me by now...' He understood a film isn't a beauty contest but an arc – an arc that takes 120 minutes from beginning to end [...]

Joel Cox. He likes natural light. He loves shadow. He always says, 'You don't need to see all the details.' Equally, he also thinks you don't have to hear every single line of dialogue perfectly. The public is on your side. They are not stupid and they can understand actions. So you can be subtle. Let the viewer use their imagination. You don't have to saturate every image with light so everything is visible [...]

Tom Stern. There are situations, particularly with lighting, where something can be ruined in two seconds. With Clint, who likes to have a certain fluidity and to also use a Steadicam [a stabilized hand-held camera], we generally just use a single source to light a scene, which allows the actor to move around anywhere in the shot and be free and spontaneous [...]

This is an extract from 'L'atelier Eastwood' ('Eastwood's studio'), a conversation with Joel Cox, Tom Stern and Henry Bumstead interviewed by Nicolas Saada and Serge Toubiana, *Cahiers du cinéma*, no. 549, September 2000.

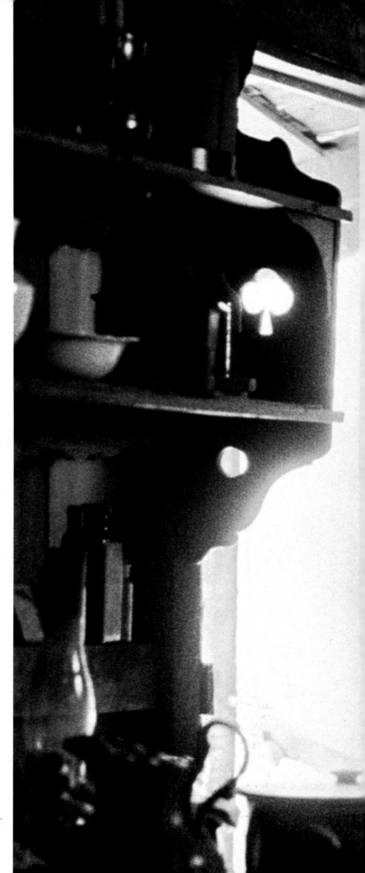

Clint Eastwood in *Pale Rider* (1985).

Elusive Origins

From *Tightrope* to *Mystic River*

Clint Eastwood in *Unforgiven* (1992).

In *Honkytonk Man*, during the course of their curious ride across America during the Great Depression, the grandfather (played by the veteran western actor John McIntire) suddenly recognizes a piece of deserted wasteland by an Oklahoma road, and tells the uncle and grandson to stop. Here he recalls a real episode in American history, evoking an image to his rapt, wide-eyed grandson. We learn that on 16 September 1893 the old man — then an adolescent (almost certainly the same age as the boy) — took part with thousands of other desperate settlers in the Cherokee Strip, the largest ever land rush held on American soil. Now in his twilight years, the grandfather's evocation of youthful hope presents us with one of the founding acts of the American West, heralding an arrival into a promised land, the dream of a clear horizon and the future. Now since turned to dust, the land has become an empty space inhabited by ghosts. The grandfather, deeply moved, ends the story by declaring, 'We ruined it, Whit, we ruined it', unexpectedly echoing the biker Captain America's words, 'We blew it', when he realizes things have gone wrong in Dennis Hopper's film *Easy Rider* (1969).

Eastwood expresses a number of his chosen themes in just this single sequence — in particular the haunting inevitability of violence in both history and America's story,[35] and a sense of things having been thrown away, of looming disaster and a gap that can be bridged only by a fantasized return to the place where trauma occurred, as if returning to a crime scene. And if this threat of violence endlessly haunts Eastwood's films, it is because he finds a perfect echo of it in himself — a reflection that both fascinates and terrifies him. The violence of history and the violence within unfold together in a grim rhythm in Eastwood's work from this point onwards (the mid-1980s to the present day), forging a cinematic space where this new monstrous conjunction can take place.

Either, or?

'We ruined it!' What did they lose? Why? Who is to blame? Whose failure was it and when did it occur? At what point in America's history did the country lurch away from its founding ideals and move into violence instead? (Or had violence always been its true ideal?).

Was it in Oklahoma on 16 September 1893, when the violation of the Native American sacred lands took place? Was it that day in 1637 when the ship, the *Desire*, bearing an American flag, set off

for Africa, inaugurating America's subjugation of Africans into slavery, eventually — over a period of two centuries — seizing against their will between 10 and 15 million human beings and taking them to the New World?[36] Or was the event that cannot be separated from the founding myth of the American West really to blame: the massacre of the Native American population?[37]

Or was it on 22 November 1963 that the United States strayed from its chosen path, when President John F. Kennedy was shot dead in Dallas? Was it on that day that the American Dream, situated somewhere between a philosophical notion of liberty, the concept of Manifest Destiny and the pursuit of happiness, finally became an impossibility? Eastwood's work seems to invite a conclusion, given the amount of times it revisits JFK's assassination (*Dirty Harry*, *In the Line of Fire*, *A Perfect World* and *Absolute Power*). Yet this traumatic moment in America's history does not seem to be the violent origin for which Eastwood is searching, because Kennedy's murder is just the most recent expression of the fork in the road when the nation's history deviated. Kennedy is only one in a recurring line of assassinated leaders, each one harking back to the next. Ultimately, the death of JFK is a screen image of a notion that remains elusive — the perfect actualization of an obsession about the origins of violence that is forever nameless. It is a blank, an absence that leaves America in a state of confusion each time this nameless act recurs in some new form, leaving nothing but an imprint in its wake, a vision of disaster and destruction.[38]

A human time bomb

Eastwood's obsession with the origins of violence also prompted a meditation on, conversely, the violence of our origins — so much so that the two themes merge together, each becoming a definition for the other in his work. Eastwood used the narrative format of the western to revisit this past, because as America's most historical genre, it is capable in its idealized form of a location and restitution of the fossil remains of some earlier and more decisive point in history, helping to illuminate the present as a result. *Josey Wales* was deliberately released in the bicentennial year (1976) of the American Revolution (1776) and Eastwood chose to situate one of the most terrible scenes in *Unforgiven* (1992) on 4 July, the anniversary of American independence. The confrontation between Sheriff Little Bill Daggett (Gene Hackman) and the appropriately named English Bob (Richard Harris) features an episode of sadistic punishment, carried out in the name of the law, to symbolically link the scene's crazed violence and murderous rage to the very act that brings about the birth of a nation.

Like a strange sign or perfect recurrence of the violence that emanates from some archaic and unlocatable point in history, images of African-American Rodney King being beaten up by the police appeared in the media in March 1991 (the following year the acquittal of the four LAPD officers provoked violent riots in Los Angeles), during the pre-production stages of *Unforgiven*, confirming to Eastwood the necessity of his film (shot during August–November 1991) as well as underlining the tragic timelessness of its themes. In the same way, Eastwood's character in *Unforgiven*, William Munny, cannot escape his nature. His repentance turns out to be a fragile house of cards when his inner demons return. Like the shadowy light he used for these stories, Eastwood's pessimism gained ground in these later works and now takes centre stage. Munny sees the small community he has created around him break apart, signalling that Eastwood's 1970s dream about community has become a mirage. It has been replaced with a sense that a bad ending is the only outcome and violence is like a human bomb, ready to go off at any time and impossible to defuse. As Butch Haynes was to also demonstrate in *A Perfect World*, Sheriff Little Bill Daggett in *Unforgiven* shows that violence constitutes a history without end, fated to continually repeat itself. He is a man who has violence in his being, it moves through him — even as he recognizes it he lets it continue to arise (as in his refusal to properly punish the two wrong-doers at the beginning), giving it life and inadvertently reproducing it through the very means he employs to try and stop it. He relies on it like an addiction and it always returns to him like a boomerang. He lives by it and he dies by it, not knowing any language other than its harsh terms.

Opposite page, left:
echos of John F. Kennedy's assassination in Wolfgang Petersen's *In the Line of Fire* (1993).

Opposite page, right:
Absolute Power (1997).

Below: Clint Eastwood and Morgan Freeman in *Unforgiven* (1992).

Little Bill can be seen as Eastwood's own historical comment on the character of Harry Callahan of thirty years before. Spanning a history of a hundred years (1881–1971), Sheriff Little Bill is the ancestor of Inspector Harry, his model and archaeological form. Both characters represent the law but they walk a tightrope, living on the borderline between morality and immorality, drawn irresistibly to cross back and forth over an invisible line in the name of some irrepressible and pathological pleasure. In this way, the scene in which the bounty-hunter English Bob receives a very public beating from Little Bill 'in the name of the law' corresponds to the 'immoral' torture Harry inflicts on Scorpio in the Kezar Stadium. We saw how Siegel, the director, expressed his own distance from and disagreement with Harry's actions in one single and masterful shot. Eastwood also uses various shots to make a comment at the finish of his own violent sequence in *Unforgiven*. At the end of the beating

scene where the continuous sound of Little Bill's blows fills the soundtrack, as English Bob lies on the ground, Eastwood suddenly presents us with a wide shot of Gene Hackman (with an American flag visible in the frame), then just as quickly presents us with a close-up of the actor's face, shifting back and forth between the two images. The sequence combines distancing and proximity, capturing the character from afar so that he appears like a staggering drunkard but also offering closer shots of his haggard face, where the traces of a kind of pleasure taken in the acts of violence are still perceptible. It is clear that Little Bill has not fully returned from the forbidden journey into his own darkest impulses.

From father to son, between friends

A Perfect World: the title tells you what could have been and what is not. In fact, Butch Haynes is a dangerous criminal who has escaped from prison,

Opposite page: Frances Fisher
(centre) in *Unforgiven* (1992).

Below: Gene Hackman in
Unforgiven (1992).

Following pages:
T. J. Lowther and Kevin Kostner in
A Perfect World (1993).

taking a young boy hostage while on the run. The criminal strangely fulfils the young kidnapped boy's wish for a father who has earlier abandoned him. And Haynes is also a man in need of a father, the one who abandoned him by forgetting to 'take' him when he also left. This neat dovetailing means that the kidnap provides a form of double fulfilment — both a final bid for freedom and a first outing into the world. Haynes sees himself in the child and the child can finally live out a fantasy of making contact with his absent father. The image of the father is very clear in Eastwood's work and, as one of his central themes, fathers litter his films. Real ones, fake ones, they turn up as strange educators, uncles of America, irresponsible conduits and physical presences that are instruments of guidance.[39] They herald initiations into extreme situations or they try to establish ties when it is almost too late, at the intersection of a life and a death, affording moments of grace and violent emotion that sometimes even border on eroticism or incest (for instance, the shocking sequence in *Absolute Power* where the young woman discovers that her father has taken photos of her unaware). His fiction can have a documentary aspect and sometimes appears to bear the tangles of his private life, exploring initiations and, in some of the works, acts of reparation, as if Eastwood, through his characters, is trying to make up for lost time, reverse what has happened and wipe away the mark of an origin that is unknown but still real, lost but still alive.

As well as initiations on a knife's edge, we also see during the period from *Honkytonk Man* to *A Perfect World*, a darkening of mood, a more sombre sky in the filmmaker's world. In *A Perfect World*, our two fugitives' journey is marked by a violence that runs through all their exchanges. It infiltrates every situation, contaminating everything in the way in which it is constantly projected and endlessly reproduces itself, similar to the toxic transference of evil in *Mystic River* (2003). Violence is slowly working away, quietly and gently, eating away at things. Ultimately, it is transmitted from one to another, like a gun being passed on. The young boy, Phillip, aged eight, kills his first man — Butch, in fact, who had carried out the very same act when he was the boy's age (like Little Bill in *Unforgiven*, his own violence kicks back at him). The history of violence does not hark back to some point in

Child's play
A Perfect World

Having escaped from prison, Butch and Terry are on the run and arrive in a peaceful town where everyone is still asleep. They separate for a moment and Terry breaks into the only house where he can see a light on. He pushes over a woman he comes across and strikes her eight-year-old son, who rolls into the corridor from the force of the blow. In the next shot, Butch appears and hits Terry, who drops his revolver. Butch (Kevin Costner) now turns towards the child (T. J. Lowther) – and it is at this point, right in the middle of this sequence, that *A Perfect World* really begins.

What does Butch do? He gets down to the level of the child, asks him his name and also asks him to pick up the gun for him. The scene isolates the man and the boy from everything else: they are united by the space of the corridor and its line of convergence, and separated from the child's mother and Terry, in their own detached world of shot reverse shots. Straightaway, Butch defuses the trauma of the intrusion by repeating his request as a game. He suggests Phillip pick up the revolver, point it at him and say 'Stick 'em up!', allowing the child to get his revenge and be the man of a house with no father. The revolver becomes a toy gun and the scene a game of 'cops and robbers'. Eastwood's choice of music and the setting provide a perfect backdrop for the powerful moment that arises at this point in the film. We also see a child's drawing on the wall, behind Phillip, as if to signify that we have gently moved into another world.

What is Butch up to? He is trying to smooth over and erase the child's shock. The revolver has become a toy and the world of childhood has been restored by a father who has seemingly fallen out of the sky. When Phillip stutters, 'Stick 'em up', Butch's face lights up and he says, 'Perfect', and in the reverse shot, we see traces of a proud smile on the boy's face. Suddenly we are in a perfect world. The beauty and folly of Butch's character lies in this wish to repair childhood, both Phillip's and his own. He wants to restore murdered pasts and heal the open wounds created by the violence of men – a violence he knows all too well because it is a violence that belongs to him, comes from his childhood, he has it in his blood, making him part-perfect-father and part-ogre. Violence seems to permeate Butch's actions and defensive body and it is from Butch, a man who appears heaven-sent, that the young boy Phillip will learn about good and evil in equal parts.

What is really happening in the film here? The 'stick 'em up' game initially disarms the film's introductory violence but also serves as a powerful premeditation or rehearsal for the violence that will follow, underlining Butch's unconscious knowledge about the unstoppable reality of violence, eternally passed on from one human to the next. At this point, as a game, he arms the little boy, but later it will be the little boy that kills him. We are watching a game of role-play, a motif for unconscious behaviour in the film. Phillip will kill his 'father' Butch, who also killed a man when he was the same age as the young boy. The film takes us full circle (Butch, when he is lying dying in the grass, recalls scenes from his life). His end takes him to his beginning. Nothing can be done. Things will always repeat themselves and a perfect world can never exist because violence will always reign, merciless to the end.

Left: Kevin Costner and T.J. Lowther in *A Perfect World* (1993).

Opposite page: Marcia Gay Harden in *Mystic River* (2003).

Following pages: Sean Penn in *Mystic River* (2003).

time immemorial when a man came across a bear and killed it out of self-defence, but it is simply the story of a man who killed a man who killed a man … And so Eastwood's greatest films have good reason to plunge right into the darkness (profoundly so in *Mystic River*) and this darkness, bit by bit, begins to encroach on the shots themselves, casting shadows on his characters' faces and inhabiting the scenes. In fact, from the beginning of the 1990s, Eastwood's work acquired an almost anthropological certainty that nothing could be done to break the violence deeply embedded in man. It is a virus that cannot be destroyed.

Ten years after *Unforgiven* and *A Perfect World*, the sombre and cold *Mystic River* completed the harrowing trilogy. One need only describe the film's final sequence, which appears like the last point of a journey that the whole of Eastwood's work has undertaken — even, it could be said, a metaphysical meditation on it all. At the heart of a little community in a run-down Boston neighbourhood, three boys — Jimmy, Sean and Dave — grow up bearing the near-suffocating guilt and burden of a terrible secret, the kidnap and rape of Dave by an adult disguised as a cop, which brought about a violent end to their childhood. Years have since gone by and Jimmy (Sean Penn), now the local hard man of the street, intends to commit a crime to avenge the murder of his daughter, Katie. He makes a kind of premeditated mistake by accusing and killing Dave (Tim Robbins), not the actual murderer of his daughter, in order to offer him a way of erasing a crime of a different and more ancient provenance, so that he can be done with an unbearable past. The film's last sequence, set on Columbus Day, has Jimmy and Sean (Kevin Bacon) — now a detective on Katie's murder case and aware of the false accusation and murder — come face to face with each other on their childhood road, each on separate sides of the street but essentially bound together in dark complicity. In a reverse angle shot, Sean points an imaginary revolver at Jimmy, who just shrugs, then puts his dark sunglasses on and applauds the passing parade. This simple gesture of impunity on the part of Jimmy and the one of powerlessness from Sean says everything we need to know: a wordless sharing of a crime and a secret understanding. Their insane pact of silence is the only testament to a violence that has loomed out of their childhood and definitively sealed the fate of the one whose innocence has always been unbearable, Dave.

Terra incognita

In this scene one witnesses the most moving aspect of Eastwood's cinema: the blindness at the heart of man, a blindness and consequent violence that endlessly repeats itself and is the central subject of Eastwood's work. Even after nearly forty years of working as a filmmaker he is always ready to re-explore man's dark origins — the three boys of *Mystic River* staring into the mouth of the drain that is swallowing all their baseballs, like a shadow's mouth; or, again, the black abyss of a shattered windscreen (*True Crime*, 1999). Eastwood's meditation on darkness and blindness also explains the different directions he has pursued and still pursues: from film noir to war films, his Darwinian man-ape comedies (the famous orangutan), the African hunting film, the westerns, the road movies and the melodramas, as well as the journey right into the soul of jazz (*Bird*) and his studies of the Deep South (*The Beguiled*, *Tightrope*, *Midnight in the Garden of Good and Evil* and *A Perfect World*). Eastwood continues to feel his way around this blindness, throwing his net as wide as possible in terms of subject matter, to try and capture the whole truth of our origins, recasting his net constantly. He undertakes a blind search for something that cannot be named, which can only be moved around, perhaps to shed a little light, to reveal glimpses of effects, but never a source — because it is one thing to talk about the violence of history but another to try and talk about the violence within man. And so John Wilson (Eastwood) in *White Hunter, Black Heart* (1990) is driven to track the African elephant, an almost prehistoric animal, like the mythical white whale of *Moby Dick*. Wilson wants to know something but he does not know what, and he has no way of understanding or naming the thing he is searching for, other than to confuse it with the African continent, the *terra incognita*.

The Other is 'I'

By searching 'blindly' in this way, in an attempt to cancel out this unlocatable historical origin of violence, Eastwood seems to be confessing, using the subject matter of his films, that his never-ending inquiry into evolutionary development is a personal source of fascination for him — his first known American ancestor lived in New Jersey in 1848. This also explains the dual resonance of his films in the

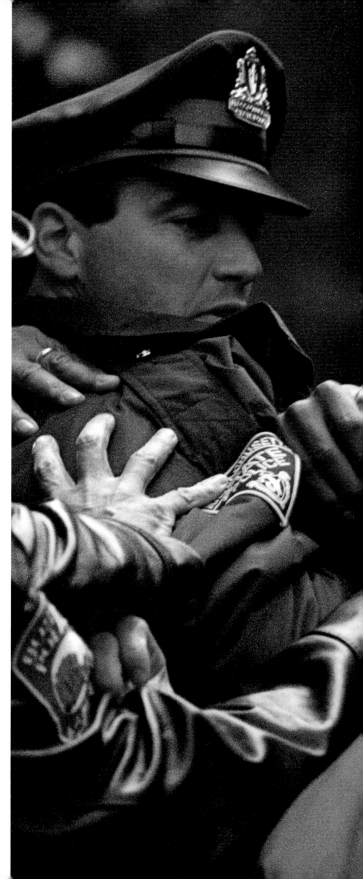

way they explore both personal and national history, the events of one used to reflect the other.

It is also a given in Eastwood's films that violence is always located in the Other: Scorpio in *Dirty Harry*, the serial killer in *Tightrope* (1984), Mitch Leary alias Booth (John Malkovich) in *In the Line of Fire*, President Richmond (Gene Hackman) in *Absolute Power* (1997) and Buddy Noone (Jeff Daniels) in *Blood Work* (2002). However, this simple distribution of character traits, this separation between his protagonists and violent Others is not as straightforward as it appears. At the beginning of *Dirty Harry* the sequence is shot so that Eastwood's first appearance on screen is linked with the first murder, creating for a fraction of a second an illusion (or truth?) of similitude between the murderer and his pursuer, like a double 'I'. During the film, Harry and Scorpio seem to be associated with various symbols that relate them to each other: Scorpio's rifle with telescopic sight compared with Harry's dark glasses; the peace and love sign on the murderer's belt as opposed to Harry's San Francisco police badge. At the end of the film, Harry throws away this badge in a gesture that was to provoke a rash of misinterpretation then and for a long time afterwards. In fact, this is the moment when the character is able to demonstrate an inner critical awareness about his own behaviour that reflects the more distanced view of both the man who plays him (Eastwood) and the film's director (Siegel). This is the moment in which Harry shows himself not worthy of being on the right side of the law because he has tipped so far into the realm of the

Other, the ghost that haunts the film and the surface upon which Harry can project his own unarticulated death wish.

By jettisoning his police badge, Harry irrevocably sentences and condemns himself.[40] Above all, his gesture is an admission that there is no difference between himself and the killer, who up until then had helped him hang on to reason and the point at which to draw the line — the means by which he could define himself in relation to an Other. In Eastwood's films the violence of the Other has always served as a screen (a smoke screen?) onto which projection can take place. It mirrors the main character. Booth (also the name of the man who assassinated Abraham Lincoln), of *In the Line of Fire*, is able to detect with an almost acute sensitivity the guilt that lies within the man who is pursuing him, echoing back poisonous insinuations on the phone to Frank Corrigan (Eastwood) and revealing intimate thoughts to him that even Corrigan cannot articulate about himself. Booth manages to do this to such a degree that Corrigan believes he is hearing himself talk when Booth talks about the day 'we' killed Kennedy. The Other is just an interior voice and in a sense 'Booth' does not exist — he is a double, one part of a divided personality, a second 'I' who serves to illuminate and reveal a person in his entirety. This is taken to its logical extreme in *Tightrope*,[41] where the 'bad character' barely exists, other than as a nondescript figure, a figment or alternative version of the cop and his own desires. Through the course of the film, Eastwood's character is slowly brought to a mirror to see the truth of his own violence — not only his own 'deviant' sexual impulses, but what lies beneath them, the death wish, the ultimate and taboo form of pleasure that fantasizes the reversal of cop and murderer. In all of his films, Eastwood has only ever acted versions of himself.

That evil may live

In 2002, Eastwood directed the film *Blood Work*. Regarded as one of his lesser films and a little preposterous in the way it exaggerates character and story, it does, however, relate killer and protagonist in a unique fashion. They complement and react to each other in unprecedented ways because, in a sense, by killing a victim who becomes an organ donor to the Eastwood character, his pursuer, the murderer gives him a new heart. Because of the murderer, the former cop has come out of retirement and is in fact dependent on him: the killer is his *raison d'être*. The Other is always one's most intimate enemy, linked to one's psyche, part of a community of the selves that exist in a person. One's alter ego is just another 'one' of us, an expression of the shadow part of our selves, which must necessarily exist to ensure the monstrous completeness of the human mind.

Eastwood exposes this dark side and drive, and seems to be filming through a two-way mirror — the true nature of the film screen. This can be seen in the deep murkiness of Surtees' shots, a dark hall of mirrors like a filmic gate that is intimate and forbidden. All the elements that make up Eastwood's attitude, both as actor and director — such as his 'cool', his minimalism, his refusal to analyse his films, his taste for concealment, the invention of an Other, the palpable inner tension within him — reveal a both conscious and unconscious strategy at play in his work, an exposure but also a cancellation of the traces of his true motives and an act both uncovering and concealing as a story advances. In brief, the films allow freedom to play out impulses through cinematic imagination.

As *Blood Work* approaches its denouement, Buddy Noone, the film's insane murderer, verbalizes the mysterious twinning of their selves in the story by shouting at the Eastwood character: 'Because that's us, Terry. That's you and me. It's us. We were meant to be. We're Cane and Abel. Kennedy and Oswald.' What if it was Lee Harvey Oswald and not Kennedy that had always fascinated Eastwood?

Opposite page: Clint Eastwood in *Blood Work* (2002).

Below: Clint Eastwood and John Malkovich in Wolfgang Petersen's *In the Line of Fire* (1993).

'The Bird of Time'

From *Heartbreak Ridge* to *Million Dollar Baby*

Clint Eastwood with Forest Whitaker and
Diane Venora on the set of *Bird* (1988).

Looked at retrospectively, Eastwood's success seems the product of a kind of empiricism informed by intuition, method and a patient working out over many years. Even if some of his films have proven to be commercial or aesthetic failures for him, because they are haphazard or lazily executed (*Pink Cadillac*, 1989; *The Rookie*, 1990), or just plain lifeless, like the last gasp of a film in the *Dirty Harry* series (*The Dead Pool*, 1988), Eastwood's cinematic work has developed in a unique way since the middle of the 1980s. Unconstrained by any need to prove himself commercially or be influenced by studio research on audiences and statistics, Eastwood has increasingly turned out works of exceptional artistry in an industry seemingly concerned only with entertainment. He has remained obsessively stubborn in his need to continue a process of exploration. The recognition he has received, along with the longevity, consistency and sheer regularity of his work, has rendered him immune to the vagaries and fashions of the Hollywood system. For over forty years Eastwood has created a very modern body of work, regarded as 'classic', now that time has elapsed.

In fact, Eastwood's cinematic art has never shied away from the process of time, whether that is the passing of time or time past, the time that remains, the time returned to us in dreams, in flashbacks, the black and white time of past eras, and the time at the heart of stories that come full circle. Finally his films also reflect what the invention of cinema ultimately gives us — the ability to preserve the living (by filming them), occasionally bringing back the dead or even permanently fixing them in our imaginations, even as film also reveals the body's ageing process and captures death quietly at work.

The pleasure principle

In *A Perfect World*, while they are on the road, Butch Haynes explains to a very young Phillip that, with a little imagination, all cars are more than simple vehicles. They are really time machines, able to leave the past in the rear mirror and, with a touch on the accelerator, travel to a future in the windscreen, or stop in the present by bringing the car to a standstill. Butch's description could be that of a film played out on an edit bench, able to fast forward, rewind and pause on an image. Are we touching on Eastwood's cinematic art here? A machine that can play with time? Yet it is only ever one linear sequence of time, as the film *A Perfect World* plays out, ultimately revealing that this parallel

Mario Van Peebles and
Clint Eastwood in
Heartbreak Ridge (1986).

world will be cancelled out. Yet Butch's fantasy image is one that holds as a description and even tells us about Eastwood's true subject matter. In *Heartbreak Ridge*, Eastwood's character, Sergeant Highway — a monolithic and muscular serviceman, seemingly impervious to time and whose conservatism literally acts like some kind of self-preservation agent — suddenly surprises his ex-wife by revealing an inner anxiety that can be understood as a commentary on his whole life: 'I just want it to end as right as it was when I started.'

The Eastwood of *Heartbreak Ridge* is in the same vein as his Bronco Billy character, both with big dreams of starting over but always believing that time will bring around the same experiences, as if time is cyclical and never a progression or evolution. If we missed the bus the first time round, we will be given another chance, and so each person, even a nation, can create a new future for themselves. This is called, quite rightly, a fiction. A perfect world. Time in a film 're-presents' another reality, tamed and fashioned to our will, rewritten, fast-forwarded or rewound. Time will make a comeback to suit our ends and Sergeant Highway makes one too in *Heartbreak Ridge*, experiencing victory and the applause of a crowd of extras when his boys are back on the tarmac. Yet this is a false victory,

cinema's sound and light show, which insists on a notion of dispossessed time, always available and ready to be used. The real victory we have here is that of Hollywood.[42]

Similarly, the screenplay for the film *In the Line of Fire* displays a kind of ingeniousness and magnanimity in the way it offers one of the unlucky bodyguards at JFK's assassination, thirty years on, nothing less than an opportunity to change the course of history and the perfect narrative set-up: a second chance to rescue an American president. And in *Absolute Power*, Eastwood's other presidential fiction, a 'super-burglar' catches the incumbent of the White House in the middle of committing a crime — *in flagrante delicto* — and, as a result, decides to singlehandedly overthrow the powers that be, so that American history — that of Lincoln and Jefferson — and his own character's relationship with his daughter, can be put back on the right track. The burglar's utopian project in *Absolute Power* is essentially the same as the one undertaken by the thief in Robert Bresson's film, *Pickpocket* (1959): Police Superintendent: 'In short, you're a sort of useful thief then, a beneficial one? My dear friend, that is a world turned upside down.' The pickpocket: 'Since it is already upside down, might it not turn things the right way up.'

But when it comes to turning time upside down, reversing it, even reprogramming it, the prize surely goes to Eastwood's *Space Cowboys* (2000) and its celebratory delight in fabricating a different world, offering the audience a masterpiece in retroaction. The film follows four old hotheads who are grandfathers and ex-NASA test pilots from the Daedalus space project. Left behind on that fateful first journey to the moon, they now find themselves some forty years later finally offered the chance to go into space. Eastwood clearly knows what he is doing here with the film's over-the-top concept. His image of the old pops' space shuttle flying upside down and backwards to avoid the moon's orbit underlines his deliberate reversal of time and the order of things. And as a classic contrarian, Eastwood has always had a taste for the fantastical because simple one-off linear stories cannot accommodate the dream of a second version, a parallel version that shadows how things turn out. Like his astronauts training in simulated environments, Eastwood conceives of *Space Cowboys* as some kind of immense time-space simulator, giving his characters a second go and creating a strange mixture of different elements so that those forgotten by history can be brought back. And once they are let loose in 'real' space, Eastwood's grandfathers experience weightlessness, but it is weightlessness on Eastwood's terms, which means time has been paused — in other words, we are in utopian time.

A work of time

Fantasy (fiction) is a form of pleasure and a denial, even the pleasure of denial: the denial of reality, of lost moments, of what has been wasted, even the denial of time itself, a dream of wiping the slate clean so that, more than just reinstating some earlier moment in time, a repaired and restored reality can come into being. It is a moment of time that has been simultaneously considered and cancelled out. We see this process of restoration occurring in *Sudden Impact* (1983), when Sondra Locke returns to the town where she and her sister had been raped. She has come back to exact revenge on the rapists but, in some kind of imaginary recovery of past time, she also spends her time fixing up the wooden horses of an old merry-go-round at the town's fairground. Again, in *Midnight in the Garden of Good and Evil*, another act of restoration: a small

71

painting is painted over and an older subject matter is made invisible to all save an X-ray machine — but, as the owner of the painting says, 'I rather enjoy not knowing.'

Right from the beginning, Eastwood's art employed strategies and tactics to play with filmic time, making it clear to the audience that it was doing so. In Leone's films, his Man with No Name character has mastery over others but he is also able to master time, distance and speed.[43] Equally, his character in *The Outlaw Josey Wales* seems possessed of a Native American ability to magically move around or suddenly appear in shot, a talent the pastor in *Pale Rider* takes to an almost supernatural degree. From early on, Eastwood's cinematic image seems to die and be repeatedly reborn — returning from the dead, disappearing and then suddenly coming back more strongly in a kind of totemic form, as a result of absence. More than invincibility, his characters demonstrate a kind of incorruptibility. In *Blood Work* the character is given a new heart and a second wind, in *A Fistful of Dollars* he has a bullet-proofed body and in *The Gauntlet* (1977) he drives an armoured bus. He is also untouchable in the cockpit of his supersonic plane in *Firefox* and again in his astronaut paraphernalia in *Space Cowboys*. In *Absolute Power* he defuses an electronic alarm with two seconds to spare and in *Midnight in the Garden of Good and Evil* it seems that time itself has stopped. The latter offers a new form of weightlessness, as if the southern town of Savannah, secluded from the world, lives as an unreal community, miraculously sheltered from history's dramas. It is a strange pot-pourri of different eras, like the flowers in a hothouse or a miniature world in a bottle, as if Eastwood is offering us here his own version of the story of *Brigadoon* (1954) and its legendary village, frozen throughout eternity except for one day each century.[44]

On the one hand, Eastwood's form of cinema dreams (without any illusions) of communities that heal and also offer fictional returns, whether it is back in time, to one's self, or to origins, in an attempt to stop failure and catastrophe and master time's effects, to go back so that one can be ready this time round. But there is another Eastwood that knows that the only power one finds from looking backwards — in fact, the only thing that ever comes back to us, like a story coming full circle or the mysterious, never-ending Möbius strip — and possibly the only thing over which time has no power, is the relentlessness of violence itself. Time moves forwards, mapping things out, never turning back, indifferent in the face of all attempts to go against it. Paradoxically then, time is also a violence and what is ruined in its wake will always persist in that state because the tear or wound it creates can never heal. It is easy to visualize — and certainly Eastwood's films give us plenty of opportunities — that the fabric of time is being restored, sewn back together (the equivalent of the cinematic link shot), but this repair is always visible, the tear is irreparable on some level, and all cinema can do is record these irreversible changes: the gash on Josey Wales's face, bodies that wrinkle, crease or become lined (from his earliest films such as *Breezy*, which

Clint Eastwood in *Space Cowboys* (2000).

Opposite page: Kevin Spacey in *Midnight in the Garden of Good and Evil* (1997).

Following pages: Clint Eastwood and Forest Whitaker on the set of *Bird* (1988).

Pages 76–7: Meryl Streep and Clint Eastwood in *The Bridges of Madison County* (1995).

seem to anticipate this theme all the way through to *Million Dollar Baby*, 2004), Red Stovall's deathly pallor (*Honkytonk Man*), Sergeant Highway's unforgettable face (*Heartbreak Ridge*), William Munny's scarred face in *Unforgiven* and the cicatrice on Terry McCaleb's torso in *Blood Work*. *A Perfect World* seems to play out man's irreversible destiny and the ultimate impossibility of two versions of time: the perfect world and time's other, more violent form. Red Garnett (Eastwood), the old Texas Ranger, can try to chase after Butch, just as Butch chases after his childhood, but Eastwood's character will never be able to bridge the gap in time he himself inaugurated many years before when he fixed Butch's future by sending him to a youth correction centre. When finally the two men cross paths again, the die is cast: the time machine cannot undo and repair the wrongs of the past and these two realities, desired time and objective time, can never be synchronized. Desired time is anti-time — this is the way through which cinema preserves, repairs, exhumes and resuscitates lost childhoods, dead presidents or even a long-ago four-day love affair in the summer of 1965 (*The Bridges of Madison County*). And yet, real or objective time — the art of rendering time's inexorable effects — also comes within cinema's domain. This encompasses the ageing of bodies, the death of Butch, the unstoppable execution of a death-row prisoner (*True Crime*)[45] or the tragic decline of Charlie 'Bird' Parker.

The reality principle

Bird (1988) is a work that strives to go back in time to an origin that even the story cannot explain, but there is no Rosebud[46] here, no mysterious clue as to Charlie Parker's mode of life. Going back in time coherently, to some form of beginning, becomes an impossible journey in this particular film by Eastwood, who makes the film endlessly erase its tracks in a way not seen in any of his earlier works. The story begins at the very end of Bird's life[47] (1954—5 and the musician's very own last moments in time) and goes on to completely disrupt the normal chronology of events, even returning back to this end point later in the film as well as showing flashbacks within flashbacks.

The film deliberately loses itself in the narrative flow, presenting us with a future that precedes the past and, as a result, rejecting conventional

Crossing into another world
The Bridges of Madison County

A summer's day in Iowa in 1965. Robert Kincaid, a photographer for *National Geographic*, is tracking down a subject – the famous covered bridges of the region. In the process he comes across another – a married woman with two children, alone for a few days and dreaming of escape to another world. Eastwood's subtle and affectionate direction turns what should be just an ephemeral meeting between two people into nothing less than a celebration of the birth of love. This expertise is seen from the beginning as the Steadicam films in one smooth flow the sequence of the woman suggesting she go along with Kincaid to Roseman Bridge and deciding to get into his car, followed by the sequence of sublime cutting once our two strangers are in the car together.

Over the course of a few minutes, in the time between house and car, we witness a conversation gently begin, slowly creating a connection that in time doesn't stop. These few minutes also capture the surrounding nature, adding a certain cosmic and elemental note to the sequence and also initiating a moment when two bodies are in a space that seems protected, in a time removed from the slow ticking of mortality, as they exchange looks and their bodies inadvertently brush against each other. A quiet rhythm begins between them and, before they arrive at the third bridge, the car has already crossed two previous bridges and a passage from one state to another has occurred. The bridges create simple markers for a process that has become irreversible. As feelings begin, there is no way back across to an earlier state – the damage has been done.

The crossing over the first two bridges seems to suggest that emotion is like a movement, that we cannot say with any certainty when it begins. It comes into being because, paradoxically, it has no absolute origin that is visible and is a line made up of an infinite number of points. Yet Eastwood's cutting of the sequence and its sensitive minimalism does invite us to isolate some of these points, in the way it captures Robert and Francesca in the car, using either head-on shots through the windscreen or at an angle as they sit by side. Crucially, at this point, the characters are always filmed from the outside of the car. Eastwood uses alternating shot reverse shots that do not exclude either when focusing on the other so that from the outset they always share the shot.

It is when Francesca tells Robert that she was born in Italy, in Bari to be precise, that we see a change in the camera's position. Eastwood uses his character Robert's surprise – as he tells her he knows Bari and spent time hanging around there – as a linking shot to move inside the car. Although still filming them from a sideways angle, the camera is now by the steering wheel when it films Francesca and on the dashboard for shots of Robert. Now more intimate, their conversation begins to flow, taking on character and nuance as the editing and pulse similarly speed up. This tightening of the shots endures, keeping the surrounding nature at bay, out of shot but not absent, in fact still very much there. As they drive onto the second bridge, the camera suddenly takes on a completely new point of view, from high above, looking down on the car, moving in an enveloping, protective and conscious way. Under this eye without name, under our own eyes as well, a 'photosynthesis' is slowly taking place.

Left: Meryl Streep and Clint Eastwood in *The Bridges of Madison County* (1995).

Opposite page: Clint Eastwood and Morgan Freeman in *Million Dollar Baby* (2004).

linear form or narrative and substituting musical form instead. This allows it to avoid the usual biopic formula of rise and fall, an ascending curve as someone achieves glory followed by descent. Bird never experiences one state without knowing the other, as ascent and descent are presented together, are even enclosed within each other, giving the character a kind of grandeur in his downfall and collapse because of the lightness (of a bird?) of his moments of glory. Forest Whitaker sums up this paradox perfectly in the way the heaviness of his body contrasts with the levity of his performance. We are in an upside-down world and an elliptical style that oscillates around various events like the shattered line of a sound wave, perfectly echoing the F. Scott Fitzgerald quotation that Eastwood uses (a first in his work) at the beginning of the film: 'There are no second acts in American lives.' And as the director of *Rebel Without a Cause* (1955), Nicholas Ray, whose own life descended into irreparable disaster, also said at the end of his own life: 'There is no second chance, not in cinema or our own very brief existences.'[48] Does this really mean that we have just one chance?

In *Million Dollar Baby* the stakes are high for Maggie Fitzgerald (Hilary Swank): she must learn to count on a one count as she hits the punch bag, because there is just this *one* chance as the film plays out. Almost too old, she can make only one attempt at living life as a champion, even if her old trainer has dreams for her and for him of a miraculous comeback, for an end that is as good as the beginning. But Eastwood only gives this character one chance, going against the classic Hollywood denouement, seemingly now a given, that believes in a second chance, a victorious comeback, a new departure and a final redemption. Here the filmmaker seems to be saying that no one can escape the merciless law of time... and yet there is always a stolen moment of weightlessness, the time containing a Charlie Parker solo filmed by Eastwood, a sequence of time that can fly with 'The Bird of Time', a moment of free jazz, a moment in Birdland.

So, finally, what is an image?

Eastwood offers us a range of films that are each like
a note he plays on an instrument, leaving us wonder-
ing if this is his final film, but also reminding us, as
a supreme and even haunted filmmaker, that he is
really just playing us one long and glorious melodious
piece of music, sometimes joyful, sometimes sombre,
always brushed by the wings of 'The Bird of Time':

> 'Come, fill the Cup, and in the Fire of Spring
> The Winter Garment of Repentance fling:
> The Bird of Time has but a little way
> To fly — and Lo! the Bird is on the Wing.'[49]

Ultimately it will always be time that will
define a body of work because real time is the very
element over which that same work has no real
power. But is this really the case? What does cinema
really do? Or to come full circle: what is an image? A
possible answer: it is the paradox of an immaterial
reality, of an idea that is stronger than even time.
And Eastwood, through his screen image and cinematic vision, has long been preparing for death,
has died many times over, is already dead, because
a moment will come when his films will be seen but
he will no longer be here. And so, in another way,
his image also tells us the opposite: Eastwood is still
alive and will live forever through his films.

Photography

Less evident than his passion for jazz in films such as *Bird*, the documentary *Thelonius Monk: Straight, No Chaser* (which he produced in 1988) or the blues in *Piano Blues* (2003), and less visible than his admiration for the art of painting ('Vanessa in the Garden' [1985] and the opening of *Absolute Power*), Eastwood's taste for photography is almost a secret pleasure, exhibited discreetly in his films but the product of far-reaching influences. To start with, the film-maker was born during an era of important American documentary photography, resulting from the Great Depression: the photographers hired by the FSA (Farm Security Administration) included Dorothea Lange, Ben Shahn, Arthur Rothstein and

Walker Evans. Half a century after Roosevelt and the New Deal, Dorothea Lange's human-ist images would of course inspire Eastwood's evocation of rural atmospheres, particular faces and the framing of certain shots in *Honkytonk Man*. Later, it was a documentary photograph (a well-publicized one) of the war, taken by Joe Rosenthal on 23 February 1945, to celebrate the taking of the Japanese island Iwo Jima, that was used to crys-tallize the stakes, tensions and dramas of *Flags of Our Fathers* (2006). Equally, the film's end credits offer the audience a som-bre slide-show of other photo-graphs taken on the devil island during the same era. Seen as an ensemble, one wonders if Eastwood is juxtaposing the

famous photograph and notion of image (representing America) against the written word of the Japanese (*Letters from Iwo Jima*, 2006), bringing together all the signs and emblems of an affront on humanity that cost over 30,000 lives.

Photography also makes an appearance in *The Bridges of Madison County*, via the char-acter Robert Kincaid, a *National Geographic* photographer and a perfect example of contradic-tion himself: is it because this eternal traveller is unable to stop at any one place that he chooses to turn places and people into fixed images? And Luther Whitney, Eastwood's dandy of a burglar in *Absolute Power*, takes secret photos of his daughter at the important stages in her

life, as if he is stalking her like a strange paparazzo covering the life of someone from afar. In his museum-like house, Whitney has displayed these photos like his own personal exhibition, almost like an imaginary storyboard of a film seen from a distance. Not only does Eastwood create one of the most moving scenes (a daughter visiting her father's private exhib-ition) in all of his cinematic work, but he is also stating, as he does in *The Bridges of Madison County*, what moves him most deeply about photography: when every-thing in this world has faded into the oblivion of death, all we have left is the unchanging power and restitution of an image. Because what is an image if not a moment of captured time, a moment of time we have regained?

Top: *The Bridges of Madison County* (1995).

Bottom left: *Flags of Our Fathers* (2006).

Bottom right: *Absolute Power* (1997).

The Presence of Ghosts

From *Flags of Our Fathers* to *Invictus*

Kazunari Ninomiya in *Letters from Iwo Jima* (2006).

Shot in the same year as *Pale Rider*'s ghostly hero and twenty years before his diptych about the war in the Pacific (*Flags of Our Fathers* and *Letters from Iwo Jima*, 2006), 'Vanessa in the Garden' (1985) is the only film Eastwood has ever made for TV. With hindsight it is clear that this episode for the NBC drama series *Amazing Stories* (1985), produced by Steven Spielberg, is a forerunner of and a model for the films Eastwood has gone on to make up to the present day.

What is 'Vanessa in the Garden' about? Set around 1895 (incidentally, the official birth of cinematography), it tells the story of an impressionist painter from New England called Byron, who brutally loses his beautiful companion, muse and model. After a night of despair about her death, he sees her, Vanessa, in the garden, as if she has returned from the dead and has stepped out of his last picture. From this point on he discovers a way to bring her back from the other side, summoning her up whenever he wishes by painting her from memory. For this ghost and love story, Eastwood was most likely influenced by Otto Preminger's *Laura* (1944), in which a detective's intense and near necrophilic obsession with a woman's image in a painting brings her back as a real 'flesh and bones'

person. 'Vanessa in the Garden' also records Byron's descent into madness and death as he too eventually crosses over into another world. In the film's last shot, both Vanessa (dressed in black) and Byron stand in front of a painting of themselves. The image has come full circle: it is a projection without end and a fantastical notion of frozen time, a suspended moment. It is also a fantasy of lovers reunited in death because it would seem, in Eastwood's world, ghosts dream of companionship too.

An army of shadows

Twenty years on and it is now old 'Doc' Bradley in *Flags of Our Fathers* who dreams of ghosts. He has had the same dream almost every night after his return from the war in the Pacific. In it, he is running around an empty battlefield trying to find a lost comrade he cannot see but who is shouting for him, an invisible body desperately crying out for help. Having worked as a naval corpsman (nurse) in the war and as an undertaker back in civilian life, each time he has the dream, he wakes up in a cold sweat, anxious that he is failing in the present in the way he has done in the past, unable to find his lost comrade and bring him back to the world of the living. The film shows how the social

83

bond — the body of men — is always dismembered by war and never fully reconstitutes itself, as the dead remain with the dead (and the forgotten dead) and the living feel guilty for being alive. The guilt of the living is made worse because the characters are required by the state and army to go on the road in a kind of 're-creation' of their combat, in order to raise money for the war effort. In doing so, they are obliged to compromise their values for the sake of the ecstatic crowds who greet them — a theatre of cruelty turned into a frenzied media circus that exists to this day. Eastwood presents *Flags of Our Fathers* and *Letters from Iwo Jima* as if they are reverse angle shots of one larger film. In *Flags of Our Fathers*, as opposed to the deathly community featured in *Letters from Iwo Jima*, we never see the three 'boys', chosen as the useful instruments of state propaganda, come together as a group or even getting on with each other. They are each more interested in

Above: Adam Beach, Ryan Phillippe and Jesse Bradford in *Flags of Our Fathers* (2006).

Opposite page: Adam Beach in *Flags of Our Fathers* (2006).

those who have been left behind on the island, or in acting on behalf of those who have died in the battle (the soldier Hayes hitchhikes his way across half the country to tell a father about the death of his son). In the end, as in Bradley's nightmare, they remain separate from each other, because no one ever fully returns from battle — not the Marines, nor *Gran Torino*'s hardened old veteran of the Korean War, who is haunted by the acts of his youth until he is freed from them by death, and not, quite literally, the Japanese general in *Letters from Iwo Jima*.

When General Kuribayashi (Ken Watanabe) arrives by plane at Iwo Jima to take up command, he believes he is still alive. In fact, he has crossed over into another world. Bit by bit, as he surveys the desolate island over the days and nights, the veil of his '*grande illusion*' is cast aside. The leader of a handful of cadaverous men, a community of ghosts without any hope of air or sea reinforcements, he

is alone, a shadowy silhouette against the world, losing his hope — it is true — but never his dignity. As the island's black sands of time run out and the enemy draws in ever closer, he comes to realize the full extent of his defeat: he has arrived into the kingdom of the dead. And so he allows himself to be buried with his own, to sink down into this world. The film follows this descent, into the shadow of an eternal ultra-black night, a dark world only ever shot through by the flash of gunfire or the grim dazzle of grenades. Long obsessed with recurring images and mirrors, Eastwood's work has slowly moved to a point where shadow becomes the fantastical reflection of lost souls, in this film and the ones that were to follow. This is what we see casting its dark light on the surfaces of the island's caves. From this forsaken landscape, a place beyond the living, where men are confined in an infernal underground, Kuribayashi decides to speak to his young son through letters that will remain long buried in this land of the dead. As a final act against the inevitability of events in this spectral world, he summons up the strength to save another 'child', the young soldier Saigo, one of the film's finest characters — somewhere between Jaroslav Hasek's Good Soldier Svejk and Stendhal's Fabrice at the Battle of Waterloo — a young man who literally cheats death, a single survivor who makes the journey back from shadow into light.

The ghost image

Among the obsessions that haunt Eastwood's most recent films, one goes back far and has never ceased to progressively permeate his work, even more so as time has created distance.[50] As a theme, it is best described as that which returns or always tries to return to the projections of our imagination or memory (cinema being the perfect art form and technique for this obsession, able to project onto a screen an image of all things that are no longer of this world, but have been captured at an earlier moment in their existence). Like Bradley and his lost friend, like the general with his army of the dead, Eastwood is exploring a revenant state — the way a distant or evanescent figure continues to haunt memories, like a ghost or revenant — before showing the impossibility of such a return and choosing, instead, to present an inverted movement towards this figure in order to unite with them. We see this in *Changeling* (2008), inspired by a terrible news story about the disappearance of a child in Los Angeles in 1928. Like the diptych it immediately followed, it is also two films in one and similarly takes up *Flags of Our Fathers*' exploration of propaganda's

Left: Angelina Jolie in *Changeling* (2008).

Above: Angelina Jolie, Jeffrey Donovan, Devon Conti and Debra Christofferson in *Changeling* (2008).

destructive effect. Both films were made during the Bush administration and what turned out to be its lies about weapons of mass destruction in Iraq. While *Flags of Our Fathers* explores the state's intense exploitation of a war photograph and their callous disregard for the true identity of the people in the image, *Changeling* examined how far the media, aided by corrupt city authorities, was prepared to go to manipulate a story in order to present an image with no relationship to the truth — that of a mother reunited with her son on a train station — even at the cost of fabricating an unnatural scene between a mother and a false child.

The second film within the first film only appears right at the end of the narrative, in the final shot, after seven years have elapsed since the story's beginning. Having gently but firmly campaigned that she will never give up hope that her son is alive, that he will reappear out of the limbo in which he exists during the playing out of the film, Christine Collins (Angelina Jolie), shot from high above, walks away from us towards Los Angeles' historical centre and carries on walking into the depths of the image until, like her son, she disappears, like the 'Pale Rider' William Munny at the very end of *Unforgiven*. Unable to fully rejoin the community of the living, 87

or make the one who has disappeared come back, she is alone between two worlds and is now a ghost herself, underlined by the fact that Eastwood could not find any trace of Christine Collins after 1935. In the film (during the sequence in the room when she says she still feels the presence of her absent son), her character reunites with her son in spirit, or her son's ghost, and she seems to fade, like him, into the surroundings. Even more than an after-life, cinema creates a space, an intermediate world, where the living and the dead can be brought close to each other, focusing attention on our own mortality in the process. Like his idea of making two films dedicated to all the dead of Iwo Jima, two films that serve as a form of burial for the fallen, Eastwood's cinematographic art consists of bringing back and embracing all the things that will never return, whether evoking a historic epoch (the Great Depression, World War II or Kennedy's assassination), a past period of a life, a golden age (the era of the studios and 'classic' cinema), a well-known name and voice (Johnny Mercer at the beginning of *Midnight in the Garden of Good and Evil*) or even a forgotten and anonymous face. Even the very act of going to the cinema can be included here, for cinema brings the dead back to life, a world of ghosts onto the screen, including Eastwood's.

Saying goodbye to Harry

What is the ghost that returns in *Gran Torino* (2008)? For a start, it is a character who has not had his fill of violence yet — the violence of history, the violence of others, the violence within a community, even violence towards himself: 'The thing that haunts a guy is the stuff he wasn't ordered to do', says the ex-soldier Walt Kowalski (Eastwood), by way of confession to a young priest about his haunting memories of the horrors of war and the crimes he committed in its name. But the real ghost in *Gran Torino* is the one that makes what initially appears to be one of Eastwood's less ambitious films the best of this last, solemn period. This ghost harks back to one of the great moments in Eastwood's cinematic history and provides an invaluable source of echoes throughout the film.

Just as *Flags of Our Fathers* attempts a non-linear story and a labyrinthine structure inherited from *Bird*, and *Changeling* submerges itself in the troubled waters of *Mystic River*, in *Gran Torino* we see a final apparition of Eastwood's Dirty Harry, as he was originally conceived by Siegel. The allusion is clear, particularly when Kowalski's large body, just before the shoot-out on the lawn, looms like some nocturnal apparition, a clear echo of Harry Callahan's immense silhouette at the end of

Sudden Impact; or again like a reversed or returned image (returned to sender, as this time it is the Eastwood character who gets shot) of the famous last sequence of *Dirty Harry*; or, finally, in the gesture Kowalski keeps making with his index finger and thumb, pretending to draw an imaginary Magnum and shoot away anyone who proves to be a pain to him. Certainly, Eastwood has never stopped exploring the deep nature of his most famous character, nor has he ever accepted, even after forty years, the accusations of racism and fascism made by Pauline Kael in her *New Yorker* article. And if Eastwood were to ask himself privately if Kael had in fact unmasked some ignored part of his self, a darker side, then what he could be seen to be doing here in *Gran Torino* is a redrawing of the character, in order to explain himself, but this time round — and very much in keeping with the times — reversing the narrative.

Opposite and following pages: Clint Eastwood in *Gran Torino* (2008).

Below: Ahney Her and Clint Eastwood in *Gran Torino* (2008).

Just as two parts make up the film *Dirty Harry* — starting with a portrait of a detective who is sure of himself, good at his job and seductive; then, in the second part, revealing a man who has lost control (exhibiting extreme violence as well as solitude and anxiety) — *Gran Torino* also presents us with a two-part story, which offers contrasting aspects of the same character. However, because the film now takes the form of a repentance narrative or confession (Eastwood's later works, such as *Million Dollar Baby*, *Changeling*, *Gran Torino*, figure a marked increase in men of the cloth), the story is reversed. First we are given a misanthropic, racist Kowalski, an insufferable reactionary and then, later on in the film, we see a more sympathetic character emerging, one who has accepted ethnic diversity and a way of the Cross. What we are seeing here is a surprising and never-ending dialogue between Eastwood the man and his famous film role, so much so that Eastwood ends up betraying Siegel's originally unflinching portrait of Harry and takes advantage of the long-ago conflation by the critic Kael of character and actor. And yet, Eastwood kills off Harry/Kowalski at the end of *Gran Torino*, maybe demonstrating a desire for imaginary repentance and perhaps quietening an unresolved contradiction within himself. A truly rare occurrence (other exceptions are Siegel's *The Beguiled* and *Honkytonk Man*), we actually see a character dying right in front of our eyes, as opposed to being sent off into the mists or the horizon. And, of course, this is not just any character: it is the character, politically incorrect, that Eastwood knows he could never really return to today. *Gran Torino* or how to kill your ghost…

In *Gran Torino* we are already seeing Eastwood addressing a contemporary America. ('We are not here in Korea', says the young priest to an out-of-date Kowalski.) Clearly, cinema has changed. Eastwood knows he is no longer making a film for the adult viewers of *Dirty Harry* but for the adolescent audiences who will watch his later films. Despite appearances to the contrary, it is clearly America that Eastwood's film *Invictus* (2009) wants to address. Released after the gloomy George W. Bush years, the United States the film is talking to is cleared of its demons, with none of the deep cinematic darkness, chiaroscuro or twilight of his earlier films, or indeed their meditations on the

unfathomable complexities of human nature and the endless cycle of man's violence. Even if it is a simplification, in the end Eastwood wants to believe in a world that is a community, reviving the utopian vision that *Bronco Billy* dreamed up on a smaller scale all those years ago. Filmed in South Africa, *Invictus* tells the story of the first years of Nelson Mandela's leadership and his tactical use of sport, in the form of rugby, to lay the foundations of reconciliation between blacks and whites (once again Eastwood is addressing the propaganda use of images, but this time for the universal good). And, this said, what finer kind of Eastwood ghost is there than Mandela, an unchanged revenant back among the company of men after thirty years of incarceration. However, this is a ghost almost for the historical record, as if Eastwood is using a black leader and the exposition of his values as some form of subliminal message about current American opinion, as if Mandela is a 'body double' for Barack Obama, that other president dedicated to the pursuit of a new world order with more humanity than others so far.

Below: Morgan Freeman in *Invictus* (2009).

Opposite page: Matt Damon in *Invictus* (2009).

A community of the living and the dead

Why has Eastwood chosen to believe in this new historical possibility, at the risk of being seen to serve the interests of a particular president and produce a film without substance concerned only to feed the audience the 'right' sentiments? The answer is that he is doing it on behalf of all those that will follow him. Here, finally, is a future for his character Saigo (*Letters from Iwo Jima*), for Thao (*Gran Torino*) and all the abused and dead children that populate his work (*Mystic River*, *Changeling*). He is offering them a chance to live in a perfect world. In the moving last shot of *Gran Torino*, Thao drives off into the distance in the film's symbolic object, the Gran Torino car that Kowalski has left him in his will — exactly like the boy drives off in the film *Honkytonk Man*. Thao has crossed over into another world, but no ghost will come to meet him (only Kowalski's voice from the grave on the sound-track) because, really, he is rejoining the constant flow of life. Saigo is not allowed to die either. The general watched over him like a father until the time would come when Saigo, in return, would be able to give the general a proper burial and go on to live beyond the horrors of war, ensuring Saigo could keep a promise he made to his then unborn child before his own departure: to be born again out of the darkness of Iwo Jima's caves, to come back alive from the kingdom of the dead. For a long time Eastwood has known that he is making the opposite journey. But from where he stands he is showing those behind him a ray of light, cinema's ray of light. And, again, from where he stands he is encouraging each generation to live by memory, to remember our fathers (and through his cinema remember him). In short, he is asking the living to live as if they are in a film, a place where the living can commune with the spirit of the dead, before they too die in a full circle that will continue forever.

Chronology

1930
31 May. Birth of Clinton Eastwood, Jr in San Francisco. Four years later, birth of a sister, Jean.

1930–45
During the Great Depression, the Eastwood family moves around California, as Eastwood, Sr goes from one precarious job to another. During the war, the family's situation becomes more stable.

1946
'It started when I was twelve years old and has continued all my life; I started by liking traditional jazz with the revival of Dixieland in the 1940s in the San Francisco area. And then I saw Charlie Parker [in 1946] and I found him extraordinary.' (*Positif*, 329, July–August 1988).

1948
Graduates from Oakland Technical High School, but not sure of his direction, spends time travelling and drifting around the country: works as a butcher in Oregon, lifeguard on Renton Beach, fireman in Sierra Nevada, a labourer in a steel works in Oakland.

Clint Eastwood with his family in the 1930s.

Clint Eastwood in the 1930s.

1951
During the Korean War (1950–3), Eastwood trains at the Fort Ord military base in Monterey. 'When I was in the Army doing my military service, it was at the same time that Huston was filming *The African Queen* and one of my additional jobs, as well as being a lifeguard, was as the film projectionist for the training films they showed to the soldiers. I could not stop playing the film *The Battle of San Pietro* (1945), one of my favourite films, which I must have seen over fifty times during my two years of military service! Having listened so much to commentary in this film, spoken by Huston, made his voice very familiar to me very early on in my life.' (*Positif*, 351, May 1990). Forty years later, Eastwood was to direct and act in *White Hunter, Black Heart*, inspired by a thinly veiled account of the making of *African Queen* and John Huston's adventurous life. **End of September.** Flying home on leave, the plane – an old Douglas – is forced to ditch into the sea. Eastwood has to swim for several miles during the night and eventually makes it to shore.

1953
19 December. Marries Maggie Johnson. They honeymoon in Carmel (California). Eastwood is twenty-three years old.

1954–8
A screen test and then a first contract as a trainee actor at Universal Studios (May 1954 – October 1955). He picks up small roles at the studios, along with a few appearances on TV, although he works as a labourer to make ends meet.

1959
9 January. Broadcast on CBS TV of the first episode of *Rawhide*, with Eastwood in the supporting role.

Clint Eastwood with two young starlets in the 1950s.

1964
17 June. Birth of Kimber Tunis, the daughter of Eastwood and Roxanne Tunis, a stuntwoman he met on the set of *Rawhide*. **April.** Eastwood takes off for Cinecittà (Rome), then Spain, to film *The Magnificent Stranger*, renamed *A Fistful of Dollars*. He can not speak Italian and Sergio Leone speaks not a word of English, but the two men understand each other and get on well.

1965
April–June. Repeats the Leone experience with *For a Few Dollars More*. **7 December.** Broadcast on CBS of the 214th and final episode of *Rawhide*, now in its eighth season.

1966
Mid-May. Begins filming *The Good, the Bad and the Ugly*. Like the two previous films, it receives poor reviews but proves to be a big success with the public in Italy, then in the United States (1968).

1967
Eastwood turns down one of the lead roles in Sergio Leone's *Once Upon a Time in the West*. Back in the United States, the actor sets up Malpaso, a production company that brings him much good fortune in his career. **November–December.** Begins shooting of *Coogan's Bluff*, directed by Don Siegel, an experienced and accomplished director. This is the first of five films they will make together, not including the small part Eastwood will give to Siegel in *Play Misty for Me* (1971), Eastwood's first film as director.

Clint Eastwood with Don Siegel on the set of *Play Misty for Me* (1971).

1968
19 May. Birth of Kyle Eastwood.

1970
Just before the filming of *Play Misty for Me* begins, Eastwood's father, Clinton Eastwood, dies at the age of sixty-three.

1971
23 July. Eastwood makes the cover of *Life*, accompanied by the by-line 'The world's favorite movie star is – no kidding – Clint Eastwood'. The star might be the public's number one, but as an actor he receives bad press. **23 December.** The Siegel–Eastwood partnership's fourth film, *Dirty Harry*, is released. This is his biggest success to date as an actor.

1972
15 January. Pauline Kael, *The New Yorker*'s film critic, attacks *Dirty Harry*, calling the film 'fascist'. **22 May.** Birth of Alison Eastwood (she was to take on roles in *Tightrope* and *Midnight in the Garden of Good and Evil*). Eastwood is proclaimed the number one star at the American box office. And, again, in 1973 and 1979.

1973
Eastwood acts in *Magnum Force*, directs his first western, *High Plains Drifter*, and then the romantic comedy, *Breezy*. At one point he thinks about giving the role of Breezy in the film to a young actress he noticed in the film *The Heart is a Lonely Hunter*, directed by Robert Ellis Miller (1968). Her name is Sondra Locke. This will be for another occasion …

1974
Eastwood turns down a part in John Guillermin's *Towering Inferno*. He gives Michael Cimino (*The Deer Hunter*, 1978) his first job as a director.

Alison Eastwood with her father on the set of Richard Tuggle's *Tightrope* (1984).

1975

September. Malpaso leaves Universal Studios for Warner Bros., heralding a long and fruitful partnership. **October.** *The Outlaw Josey Wales* begins filming, the first of seven films Eastwood makes with the actress Sondra Locke, who becomes his partner. He turns down an offer from Francis Ford Coppola to act in a film project called *Apocalypse Now*.

1978

Against the advice of his associates, he acts in *Every Which Way but Loose*, a crackpot comedy with an orangutan, which ends up being one of his biggest successes at the American box office.

1979

Shoots *Bronco Billy*. It is a commercial failure but heralds the beginnings of critical success for him.

1982

Directs and acts in *Honkytonk Man*. His son, Kyle Eastwood, plays the role of his nephew but later chooses music as his career (as a jazz bass player and as a composer for films such as *Mystic River*, *Million Dollar Baby* and the Iwo Jima diptych).

1984

May. An employee in the script department of Warner Bros., Megan Rose, comes across a screenplay called *The William Munny Killings*. She tells Eastwood about her discovery. Eight years later the screenplay becomes *Unforgiven*. Eastwood and his wife, Maggie, officially divorce. **19 December 1984 – 14 January 1985.** A full retrospective of Eastwood's work is shown at the Cinémathèque Française, Paris.

Clint Eastwood, the new mayor of Carmel, took the oath on 15 April 1986.

1985

14 May. *Pale Rider* is entered into competition at the Cannes Film Festival. The same year, Eastwood films 'Vanessa in the Garden', his only film for TV and his last film with Sondra Locke.

1986

10 April. Eastwood is elected mayor of Carmel-by-the-Sea (California). He remains in office for two years.

1987

October 1987 – January 1988. Filming of *Bird*.

1988

September. Eastwood's films are selected for the collection at the Museum of Modern Art, New York. Wesleyan University, Middletown, CT, acquires the Malpaso archive of films. **Autumn.** While Eastwood is in Rome for the premiere of *Bird*, Sergio Leone invites him to lunch. The two men had not seen each other for twenty years. With hindsight, Eastwood said he thought Leone, feeling nostalgic, had called him that day to say 'goodbye'. Secretly ill, the Italian filmmaker dies on 30 April 1989.

1989

Officially breaks up with Sondra Locke, who sells a kiss-and-tell story to the press, much to their delight. **July–August.** Eastwood goes off to film *White Hunter, Black Heart* in the United Kingdom and Africa.

1991

20 April. Death of Don Siegel. *Unforgiven* was to be dedicated to 'Sergio and Don'. 'He pushed me into directing and I pushed him into being an actor … When I saw the *Invasion of the Body Snatchers* (probably one of the two or three best B movies of all time), I realized he was a man that was able to do great things with very little … I think if I have learned one thing from Don Siegel, it is to know what it is you want to film and to also recognize when you have got it – and that is something I have not often seen happening over the years' (from the Foreword by Eastwood in Alain Silver and Elizabeth Ward [eds], *A Siegel Film: An Autobiography*, Faber & Faber, London, 1993). **26 August – 12 November.** Filming of *Unforgiven*.

1993

29 March. Oscars ceremony. Nominated nine times, *Unforgiven* is awarded four Oscars (best film, best director, best actor [Gene Hackman] and best editing). Filming and release of *In the Line of Fire* and *A Perfect World*. **7 August.** Birth of Francesca Fisher-Eastwood, Eastwood's daughter with Frances Fisher (*Unforgiven*). In 1999, the young Francesca was to play the daughter of her father's character in *True Crime*.

1994

May. President of the Cannes Film Festival Jury, which awarded the Palm d'Or to Quentin Tarantino's *Pulp Fiction*. **September – October.** Shooting of *The Bridges of Madison County* in Iowa.

1996

February. Eastwood receives a Life Achievement Award from the American Film Institute. **31 March.** Eastwood marries Dina Ruiz, a TV presenter thirty-five years his junior. **April.** He is honoured by The Film Society of Lincoln Center (New York). **June – August.** Films *Absolute Power*.

1997

May–July. Films *Midnight in the Garden of Good and Evil* in Savannah (Georgia).

1998

28 February. In Paris, Eastwood is presented with an honorary César by Jean-Luc Godard.

Clint Eastwood with Kyle and Alison at the Academy Awards in 1993.

1999

July-October. Films *Space Cowboys*.

2001

Virtual pop band Gorillaz release their first single, called 'Clint Eastwood'. In 2005, the group releases a second album, *Demon Days*, which includes a track called 'Dirty Harry'.

2002

August. *Blood Work* is released.

2004

Mystic River wins two Oscars (for best actors Sean Penn and Tim Robbins).

2005

Four Oscars for *Million Dollar Baby*: best film, best director, best actress (Hilary Swank) and best actor (Morgan Freeman).

2006

7 February. Death of Eastwood's mother, Ruth Runner Eastwood, at the age of ninety-seven.

2006 – 7

Filming and release of *Flags of Our Fathers* and *Letters from Iwo Jima*, a diptych offering two different perspectives on the bloody Battle of Iwo Jima during the Pacific Campaign of World War II.

2008

Eastwood makes *Gran Torino*, heralding his return as an actor for the first time since *Million Dollar Baby*. The film garners both critical and box-office success.

2009 – 10

After shooting *Invictus* in South Africa, Eastwood shoots the supernatural thriller *Hereafter*, starring Matt Damon, on locations in Paris and the United States.

Clint Eastwood with Jay McShann in *Piano Blues* (2003).

Filmography

ACTOR ONLY

Revenge of the Creature	1955
by Jack Arnold	
Francis in the Navy	1955
by Arthur Lubin	
Lady Godiva of Coventry	1955
by Arthur Lubin	
Tarantula!	1955
by Jack Arnold	
Never Say Goodbye	1956
by Jerry Hopper	
Star in the Dust	1956
by Charles Haas	
Away All Boats	1956
by Joseph Pevney	
The First Traveling Saleslady	1956
by Arthur Lubin	
Escapade in Japan	1957
by Arthur Lubin	
Lafayette Escadrille	1958
by William A. Wellman	
Ambush at Cimarron Pass	1958
by Jodie Copeland	
Rawhide	1959–65

TV series, broadcast on CBS from 9 January 1959 to 7 December 1965 (eight seasons, 214 episodes)

A Fistful of Dollars	1964

Per un pugno di dollari
by Sergio Leone

For a Few Dollars More	1965

Per qualche dollaro in più
by Sergio Leone

The Good, the Bad and the Ugly	1966

Il buono, il brutto, il cattivo
by Sergio Leone

Una sera come le altre	1967

by Vittorio De Sica
(fifth sketch of *Le Streghe*)

Where Eagles Dare	1969
by Brian G. Hutton	
Paint Your Wagon	1969
by Joshua Logan	
Kelly's Heroes	1970
by Brian G. Hutton	

ACTOR AND PRODUCER

Hang 'Em High	1968
by Ted Post	
Coogan's Bluff	1968
by Don Siegel	
Two Mules for Sister Sara	1970
by Don Siegel	
The Beguiled	1971
by Don Siegel	
Dirty Harry	1971
by Don Siegel	
Joe Kidd	1972
by John Sturges	
Magnum Force	1973
by Ted Post	
Thunderbolt and Lightfoot	1974
by Michael Cimino	
The Enforcer	1976
by James Fargo	
Every Which Way But Loose	1978
by James Fargo	
Escape from Alcatraz	1979
by Don Siegel	
Any Which Way You Can	1980
by Buddy Van Horn	
City Heat	1984
by Richard Benjamin	
Tightrope	1984
by Richard Tuggle	
The Dead Pool	1988
by Buddy Van Horn	
Pink Cadillac	1989
by Buddy Van Horn	
In the Line of Fire	1993
by Wolfgang Petersen	

SHORT FILM

The Beguiled: the Storyteller	1971

Format 16mm. **Running time** 12 mins.

• On the set of Don Siegel's film *The Beguiled*, Eastwood becomes a director for the first time by filming a short documentary about Siegel.

TELEVISION FILMS

Vanessa in the Garden	1985

Running time 25 mins. With Harvey Keitel, Sondra Locke, Beau Bridges, Margaret Howell.

• In 1895 in New Hampshire, an impressionist painter in despair after the death of his wife and model, finds a way to bring her back to life. Episode 9 of the *Amazing Stories* TV series.

Piano Blues	2003

Running time 1h 29.

• A documentary mixing archive images and present-day interviews with, among others, Ray Charles and Dave Brubeck. Broadcast as part of the seven-episode series, *The Blues*, produced by Martin Scorsese.

FEATURE FILMS

Play Misty for Me	1971

Screenplay Jo Heims, Dean Riesner. **Cinematography** Bruce Surtees. **Editing** Carl Pingitore. **Music** Dee Barton, Erroll Garner. **Production** Malpaso, Universal. **Running time** 1h 35. With Clint Eastwood (Dave Garver), Jessica Walter (Evelyn), Donna Mills (Tobie), Don Siegel (the barman).

• In the charming little town of Carmel, a womanizer falls into a trap laid for him by a female stalker.

High Plains Drifter	1973

Screenplay Ernest Tidyman, Dean Riesner. **Cinematography** Bruce Surtees. **Production design** Henry Bumstead. **Editing** Ferris Webster. **Music** Dee Barton. **Production** Malpaso, Universal. **Running time** 1h 42. With Clint Eastwood (The Stranger), Verna Bloom (Sarah Belding), Mariana Hill (Callie Travers), Jack Ging (Morgan Allen), Geoffrey Lewis (Stacey Bridges).

• A man without a name, who seems to have come out of nowhere, arrives in Lago, a strange town in the Far West, built by the banks of a salt lake and eaten up by a hidden guilt.

Breezy	1973

Screenplay Jo Heims. **Cinematography** Frank Stanley. **Editing** Ferris Webster. **Music** Michel Legrand. **Production** Malpaso, Universal. **Running time** 1h 47. With William Holden (Frank), Kay Lenz (Breezy), Marj Dusay (Betty Tobin), Roger C. Carmel (Bob Henderson).

• A cynical older millionaire meets a penniless young dreamer.

The Eiger Sanction	1975

Screenplay Hal Dresner, Warren B. Murphy, Rod Whitaker, from the novel by Trevanian. **Cinematography** Frank Stanley. **Editing** Ferris Webster. **Music** John Williams. **Production** Malpaso, Universal. **Running time** 2h 08. With Clint Eastwood (Jonathan Hemlock), George Kennedy (Ben), Brenda Venus (George), Thayer David (Dragon).

• A former secret agent, now an art expert and an experienced mountaineer, returns to work and a mountain adventure.

The Outlaw Josey Wales 1976
Screenplay Phil Kaufman, Sonia Chernus, from the novel *Gone to Texas* by Forrest Carter. **Cinematography** Bruce Surtees. **Editing** Ferris Webster. **Music** Jerry Fielding. **Production** Malpaso, Warner Bros. **Running time** 2h 15. With Clint Eastwood (Josey Wales), Sondra Locke (Laura Lee), Chief Dan George (Lone Watie), Bill McKinney (Terrill), Sam Bottoms (Jamie), John Vernon (Fletcher).

• It is the end of the American Civil War but one man who has lost everything, apart from his rage, will not lay down his arms. He sets off blindly on a secret but evolving mission.

The Gauntlet 1977
Screenplay Michael Butler, Dennis Shryack. **Cinematography** Rexford Metz. **Editing** Ferris Webster. **Music** Jerry Fielding. **Production** Malpaso, Warner Bros. **Running time** 1h 51. With Clint Eastwood (Ben Shockley), Sondra Locke (Gus), Pat Hingle (Josephson), William Prince (Blakelock), Mara Corday, Bill McKinney.

• A narrow-minded cop accompanies a loud-mouthed hooker on a chaos-filled journey from Las Vegas to Phoenix. When the 'weaker sex' gets hold of a gun.

Bronco Billy 1980
Screenplay Dennis Hackin. **Cinematography** David Worth. **Editing**

Ferris Webster. **Music** Snuff Garrett ('Bar-room Buddies' performed by Merle Haggard and Clint Eastwood). **Production** Malpaso, Warner Bros. **Running time** 1h 56. With Clint Eastwood (Bronco Billy McCoy), Sondra Locke (Antoinette Lily), Scatman Crothers (Doc), Geoffrey Lewis (Arlington), Sam Bottoms (Leonard).

• A cowboy at heart, a man travels with his little troupe from town to town across contemporary America, doing whatever it takes to keep alive the spirit of the American West in their Wild West show.

Firefox 1982
Screenplay Alex Lasker, Wendell Wellman, from the novel by Craig Thomas. **Cinematography** Bruce Surtees. **Editing** Ferris Webster. **Music** Donald Harris. **Production** Malpaso, Warner Bros. **Running time** 2h. With Clint Eastwood (Mitchell Gant), Freddie Jones (Kenneth Aubrey), David Huffman (Buckholz), Warren Clarke (Pavel Upenskoy).

• An outstanding pilot, who is also a traumatized Vietnam veteran, takes up service again. His mission: to infiltrate the Soviet Union and steal their ultimate weapon, an invisible-to-radar plane that flies at Mach 6 and can be steered by thoughtwaves.

Honkytonk Man 1982
Screenplay Clancy Carlile, from his novel. **Cinematography** Bruce Surtees. **Production design** Edward Carfagno. **Editing** Ferris Webster. **Music** Snuff Garrett. **Production** Malpaso, Warner Bros. **Running time** 2h 02. With Clint Eastwood (Red Stovall), Kyle Eastwood (Whit), John McIntire (Grandpa), Alexa Kenin (Marlene),Verna Bloom (Emmy).

• In the 1930s, a country singer with tuberculosis and his young nephew take to the road bound for Nashville on an unforgettable journey.

Sudden Impact 1983
Screenplay Joseph C.Stinson. **Cinematography** Bruce Surtees. **Production design** Edward Carfagno. **Editing** Joel Cox. **Music** Lalo Schifrin. **Production** Malpaso, Warner Bros. **Running time** 1h 57. With Clint Eastwood (Harry Callahan), Sondra Locke (Jennifer Spencer), Pat Hingle (Jannings), Bradford Dillman (Briggs).

• This time, Harry's bosses send him far from San Francisco to investigate a series of murders in the little town of San Paulo, where he meets an enigmatic woman.

Pale Rider 1985
Screenplay Michael Butler, Dennis Shryack. **Cinematography** Bruce Surtees. **Production design** Edward Carfagno. **Editing** Joel Cox. **Music** Lennie Niehaus. **Production** Malpaso, Warner Bros. **Running time** 1h 51. With Clint Eastwood (Preacher), Michael Moriarty (Hull Barret), Christopher Penn (Josh LaHood), Richard Dysart (Coy).

• A group of panning miners are being harassed by a local businessman who wants to eject them from their land. They are about to give up when a solitary man on horseback appears from the mountains and gives them back their faith.

Heartbreak Ridge 1986
Screenplay James Carabatsos, Dennis Hackin, Joseph Stinson. **Cinematography** Jack N. Green. **Production design** Edward Carfagno. **Editing** Joel Cox. **Music** Lennie Niehaus. **Production** Malpaso, Warner Bros. **Running time** 2h 10. With Clint Eastwood (Sergeant Tom Highway), Marsha Mason (Aggie), Everett McGill (Major Powers), Mario Van Peebles (Stitch Jones).

• Sergeant Highway, a Korean and Vietnam War veteran, who is detested by his superiors and kept at a distance by his ex-wife, is given the

job of knocking a group of shirkers into shape. Loving a challenge, he gets down to the job of transforming his band of no-goods.

Bird 1988
Screenplay Joel Oliansky. **Cinematography** Jack N. Green. **Production design** Edward Carfagno. **Editing** Joel Cox. **Music** Lennie Niehaus. **Production** Malpaso, Warner Bros. **Running time** 2h 43. With Forest Whitaker (Charlie Parker), Diane Venora (Chan), Samuel E. Wright (Dizzy Gillespie), Michael Zelniker (Red Rodney).

• Eastwood explores the life of Charlie 'Bird' Parker, the composer, saxophonist and pioneer of bebop, set against the background of 1940s and 50s America.

White Hunter, Black Heart 1990
Screenplay Peter Viertel, James Bridges, Burt Kennedy, from the novel by Peter Viertel. **Cinematography** Jack N. Green. **Editing** Joel Cox. **Music** Lennie Niehaus. **Production** Malpaso, Rastar, Warner Bros. **Running time** 1h 52. With Clint Eastwood (John Wilson), Jeff Fahey (Peter Verrill), George Dzundza (Paul Landers).

• John Wilson, an eccentric director in the 1950s, is making his new film in Africa, but his great passion for hunting elephants threatens to take over the making of his work.

The Rookie 1990
Screenplay Boaz Yakin, Scott Spiegel. **Cinematography** Jack N. Green. **Editing** Joel Cox. **Music** Lennie Niehaus. **Production** Malpaso, Warner Bros. **Running time** 2h 01. With Clint Eastwood (Nick Pulovski), Charlie Sheen (David Ackerman), Raul Julia (Strom).

• An irascible cop, forced to work with a brand new recruit, hunts down a dangerous gang leader and his sadistic mistress.

Unforgiven 1992

Screenplay David Webb Peoples. **Cinematography** Jack N. Green. **Production design** Henry Bumstead. **Editing** Joel Cox. **Music** Lennie Niehaus, Clint Eastwood ('Claudia's Theme'). **Production** Malpaso, Warner Bros. **Running time** 2h 11. With Clint Eastwood (William Munny), Gene Hackman (Little Bill Daggett), Morgan Freeman (Ned Logan), Richard Harris (English Bob), Jaimz Woolvett (The Schofield Kid), Frances Fisher (Strawberry Alice).

• The county of Wyoming in 1881. A killer, who has given up his old ways but is desperate for money, renews his links with the devil by accepting a contract to take up his gun again.

A Perfect World 1993

Screenplay John Lee Hancock. **Cinematography** Jack N. Green. **Production design** Henry Bumstead. **Editing** Joel Cox. **Music** Lennie Niehaus (and Clint Eastwood). **Production** Malpaso, Warner Bros. **Running time** 2h 18. With Kevin Costner (Butch Haynes), Clint Eastwood (Red Garnett), Laura Dern (Sally Gerber), T. J. Lowther (Phillip Perry).

• It is 1963. An escaped convict is on the run, but he takes a young boy with him on a both desperate and joyful journey, giving him a sudden taste of a world he knows nothing about.

The Bridges of 1995
Madison County

Screenplay Richard LaGravenese, from the novel by Robert James Waller. **Cinematography** Jack N. Green. **Editing** Joel Cox. **Music** Lennie Niehaus. **Production** Malpaso, Amblin, Warner Bros. **Running time** 2h 09. With Clint Eastwood (Robert Kincaid), Meryl Streep (Francesca Johnson), Annie Corley (Carolyn), Victor Slezak (Michael).

• It is 1965 in the countryside of Iowa. A married woman and a photog-

rapher passing through, meet and spend four days together, falling deeply in love. They have to part but never stop loving each other for the rest of their lives.

Absolute Power 1997

Screenplay William Goldman, from the novel by David Baldacci. **Cinematography** Jack N. Green. **Production design** Henry Bumstead. **Editing** Joel Cox. **Music** Lennie Niehaus, Clint Eastwood ('Kate's Theme'). **Production** Malpaso, Castle Rock, Columbia. **Running time** 2h. With Clint Eastwood (Luther Whitney), Gene Hackman (President Richmond), Ed Harris (Seth Frank), Laura Linney (Kate Whitney), Judy Davis (Gloria Russell).

• A master burglar discovers the United States president in a compromising situation. Now on the run, he tries to get back in contact with the daughter he never really knew, although in reality he had never really lost sight of her.

Midnight in the 1997
Garden of Good and Evil

Screenplay John Lee Hancock, from the novel by John Berendt. **Cinematography** Jack N. Green. **Production design** Henry Bumstead. **Editing** Joel Cox. **Music** Lennie Niehaus. **Production** Malpaso, Warner Bros. **Running time** 2h 30. With Kevin Spacey (Jim Williams), John Cusack (John Kelso), Jude Law (Billy Hanson), Alison Eastwood (Mandy Nicholls), The Lady Chablis (Chablis Deveau).

• A New York journalist arrives in Savannah, Georgia, and discovers an unexpected place, tucked away from the rest of the world – an intoxicating, warm but lethal little kingdom.

True Crime 1999

Screenplay Larry Gross, Paul Brickman, Stephen Schiff, from the novel by Andrew Klavan. **Cinematography** Jack N. Green. **Produc-**

tion design Henry Bumstead. **Editing** Joel Cox. **Music** Lennie Niehaus. **Production** Malpaso, Warner Bros. **Running time** 2h 07. With Clint Eastwood (Steve Everett), Isaiah Washington (Frank Beechum), James Woods (Alan Mann), Francesca Fisher-Eastwood (Kate Everett).

• In San Quentin, Oakland, an African-American on death row has only a few hours to live. Six years earlier he had supposedly killed a white woman in cold blood. A washed-up journalist decides to try and prove that he is innocent before it is too late.

Space Cowboys 2000

Screenplay Ken Kaufman, Howard Klausner. **Cinematography** Jack N. Green. **Production design** Henry Bumstead. **Editing** Joel Cox. **Music** Lennie Niehaus, Clint Eastwood ('Espacio'). **Production** Malpaso, Mad Chance, Warner Bros. **Running time** 2h 09. With Clint Eastwood (Frank Corvin), Tommy Lee Jones (William 'Hawk' Hawkins), Donald Sutherland (Jerry O'Neill), James Garner (Tank Sullivan), Marcia Gay Harden (Sara Holland).

• Four old hotheads, who missed out on their chance to go into space, get called up by NASA forty years later.

Blood Work 2002

Screenplay Brian Helgeland, from the novel by Michael Connelly. **Cinematography** Tom Stern. **Production design** Henry Bumstead. **Editing** Joel Cox. **Music** Lennie Niehaus. **Production** Malpaso, Warner Bros. **Running time** 1h 50. With Clint Eastwood (Terry McCaleb), Jeff Daniels (Buddy Noone), Anjelica Huston (Bonnie Fox), Wanda De Jesus (Graciella Rivers).

• Following a heart attack and transplant, an ancient FBI profiler investigates the death of the person who gave him his new organ.

Mystic River 2003

Screenplay Brian Helgeland, from

the novel by Dennis Lehane. **Cinematography** Tom Stern. **Production design** Henry Bumstead. **Editing** Joel Cox. **Music** Lennie Niehaus, Clint Eastwood. **Production** Malpaso, Warner Bros. **Running time** 2h 17. With Sean Penn (Jimmy Markum), Tim Robbins (Dave Boyle), Kevin Bacon (Sean Devine), Laurence Fishburne (Whitey Powers), Marcia Gay Harden (Celeste Boyle), Laura Linney (Annabeth Markum).

• In Boston, the violent death of Jimmy's daughter leads to an investigation that unearths a buried childhood trauma shared by Jimmy and his two boyhood friends.

Million Dollar Baby 2004

Screenplay Paul Haggis, from three short stories by F. X. Toole. **Cinematography** Tom Stern. **Production design** Henry Bumstead. **Editing** Joel Cox. **Music** Clint Eastwood, Kyle Eastwood. **Production** Malpaso, Warner Bros. **Running time** 2h 12. With Clint Eastwood (Frankie Dunn), Hilary Swank (Maggie Fitzgerald), Morgan Freeman (Scrap), Jay Baruchel (Danger).

• Frankie, an old boxing trainer with no future, after much hesitation takes on the training of a young woman who is filled with a rage to make it before it is too late.

Flags of Our Fathers 2006

Screenplay William Broyles, Jr, Paul Haggis, from the book by James Bradley and Ron Powers. **Cinematography** Tom Stern. **Production design** Henry Bumstead. **Editing** Joel Cox. **Production** Malpaso, Amblin, Warner Bros. **Running time** 2h 12. With Ryan Phillippe (John Bradley), Jesse Bradford (René Gagnon), Adam Beach (Ira Hayes), Benjamin Walker (Harlon Block).

• Seen from the American perspective, the bloody battle on the island of Iwo Jima during World War II is the story of a photograph that was reproduced around the world and the three flag-bearers featured in the image – heroes in spite of themselves.

Letters from Iwo Jima 2006
Screenplay Iris Yamashita, Paul Haggis. **Cinematography** Tom Stern. **Production design** Henry Bumstead. **Editing** Joel Cox. **Production** Malpaso, Amblin, Warner Bros. **Running time** 2h 19. With Ken Watanabe (General Tadamichi Kuribayashi), Kazunari Ninomiya (Saigo), Tsuyoshi Ihara (Baron Nishi), Ryo Kase (Shimizu).
• The history of the Battle of Iwo Jima seen from the Japanese side.

Changeling 2008
Screenplay J. Michael Straczynski. **Cinematography** Tom Stern. **Production design** James J. Murakami. **Editing** Joel Cox, Gary Roach. **Production** Malpaso, Imagine Entertainment. **Running time** 2h 11. With Angelina Jolie (Christine Collins), Jason Butler Harner (Gordon Northcott), John Malkovich (Reverend Briegleb), Jeffrey Donovan (Captain J. J. Jones).
• Los Angeles, 1928. A single woman lives with her son. One morning, he disappears. When, a few months later, the police insist they have found him, she refuses to recognize him as her son, although they insist that he is.

Gran Torino 2008
Screenplay Nick Schenk, Dave Johannson. **Cinematography** Tom Stern. **Production design** James J. Murakami. **Editing** Joel Cox, Gary Roach. **Music** Kyle Eastwood, Michael Stevens. **Production** Malpaso. **Running time** 1h 51. With Clint Eastwood (Walt Kowalski), Bee Vang (Thao), Ahney Her (Sue), Geraldine Hughes (Karen Kowalski).
• In a suburb of Michigan, a bilious and unashamedly racist Korean War veteran, Walt Kowalski, buries his wife. Meanwhile a family from the Hmong community – originally from Laos – move in next door.

Invictus 2009
Screenplay Anthony Peckham, from the book *Playing the Enemy* by John Carlin. **Cinematography** Tom Stern. **Production design** James J. Murakami. **Editing** Joel Cox, Gary Roach. **Production** Malpaso. **Running time** 2h 12. With Morgan Freeman (Nelson Mandela), Matt Damon (François Pienaar), Robert Hobbs (Willem), Langley Kirkwood (George).
• South Africa, 1994: Nelson Mandela, a political prisoner for nearly thirty years, has now been elected the leader of a country ravaged by forty years of apartheid and three centuries of racial segregation. 1995: South Africa is hosting the Rugby World Cup and Mandela decides to transform the image of the Springbok team as a much-hated symbol of the apartheid regime, into a focus of national reconciliation and pride.

Selected Bibliography

American History
History of the American Cinema: vol. 8, Paul Monaco, *The Sixties: 1960–1969;* vol. 9, David A. Cook, *Lost Illusions: 1970–1979;* vol. 10, Stephen Prince, *A New Pot of Gold: 1980–1989,* Charles Scribner's Sons, New York.

Howard Zinn,
A People's History of the United States: 1492 – Present,
Pearson Education Limited, Harlow, England, 2003 (first published 1980).

James Agee and Walker Evans
Let Us Now Praise Famous Men: Three Tenant Families
Mariner Books, Boston, 2001 (first published 1941).

Gilles Mora and Beverly Brannan
FSA: The American Vision
Harry Abrams, New York, 2006.

Don Siegel
Stuart M. Kaminsky
Don Siegel: Director
Curtis Books, Philadelphia, 1974.

A Siegel Film: An Autobiography
ed. Alain Silver and Elizabeth Ward, Faber & Faber, London, 1993 (with a foreword by Clint Eastwood).

Clint Eastwood
Richard Schickel
Clint Eastwood: A Biography
Knopf, New York, 1996.

Patrick McGilligan
Clint: The Life and Legend
St. Martin's Press, New York, 1999.

Robert E. Kapsis and Kathie Coblentz (eds)
Clint Eastwood: Interviews
University Press of Mississippi, 1999.

Notes

1. Jim Williams (Kevin Spacey) in *Midnight in the Garden of Good and Evil* (1997).

2. Extract from an interview with Eastwood published in *Playboy* magazine in February 1974.

3. *A Fistful of Dollars* (1964), *For a Few Dollars More* (1965), *The Good, The Bad and the Ugly* (1966).

4. In March 1933, between 11 and 12 million Americans were unemployed.

5. A suffering that at the time was revealed by humanist and militant American art. For example, photographic work by Dorothea Lange, Walker Evans and Ben Shahn, films by William Wellman (*Wild Boys of the Road*, 1933), Frank Borzage (*Man's Castle*, 1933), King Vidor (*Our Daily Bread*, 1934), John Ford (*The Grapes of Wrath*, 1940, adapted from Steinbeck's novel, 1939), and also the unflinching *Let Us Now Praise Famous Men*, a photographic record carried out by the writer James Agee and the photographer Walker Evans (1936–9).

6. Including, in this case, Bob Wills And His Texas Playboys, whose music was to be used nearly fifty years later in *A Perfect World*.

7. Quoted in Richard Schickel, *Clint Eastwood: A Biography*, Knopf, New York, 1996, p.68.

8. This description shouldn't conceal Eastwood's state of mind at the time: driven to succeed even as he faced constant rejection at the end of the 1950s, as just another freelance actor dealing with humiliating auditions at Warner, Columbia, Paramount (screen tests through a two-way mirror, etc.) and Twentieth Century Fox as well as the frustration of not being chosen for parts by the big directors of the time. In short, we see evidence of the rage that has always been within him, a certain violence that had no outlet at the time but was to later be employed in both his acting and explored in his cinematic work (*The Outlaw Josey Wales*, for example).

9. Edgar Morin, *The Stars*, Grove Press, New York, 1960.

10. Others included John Cassavetes (*Johnny Staccato*, 1959–60), Steve McQueen (*Wanted: Dead or Alive*, 1958–61), James Garner (*Maverick*, 1957–60), and also Burt Reynolds, James Coburn, Warren Oates …

11. After Leone's *Dollars* trilogy, during the filming of his next film back in the United States, Ted Post's *Hang 'Em High*, Eastwood drove the point home for those who had missed the spaghetti westerns. The film begins with a cowboy and his herd, an image that looks straight out of the *Rawhide* series, as if we are seeing the return of Rowdy Yates. But the image doesn't last, because within a few minutes he is attacked by a crazed mob, hanged and left for dead. Right after a shot from below of his dangling boots, the film's title comes into view.

12. John F. Kennedy was shot on 22 November 1963. On 28 August, in Washington, Martin Luther King delivered his 'I Have a Dream' speech calling for an end to racial discrimination. In 1964, U.S. forces officially escalated their involvement in the Vietnam War.

13. In short, the critics, reacting in an instinctively conservative way, did exactly what Baudelaire had reproached them for many years before: 'Decadent literature! – The empty words we always hear from the lips of these sphinxes without enigma, who guard the gates of the classical aesthetic' (Charles Baudelaire, *Notes nouvelles sur Edgar Poe*, 1857).

14. As early as the 1960s, *The New Yorker* film critic Pauline Kael wrote about him: 'Clint isn't an actor, so one could hardly call him a bad actor.'

15. In contrast, his role in a Italian film made up of segments, *Le streghe* (*The Witches*, 1967), directed by Vittorio De Sica, attests to his own badly expressed need at the time to broaden and develop his image. In De Sica's story ('Una sera come le altre'), Eastwood dons a suit and does comedy, playing a banker more obsessed with the ups and downs of the stock market than his wife (Silvana Mangano). Suffice to say, the film and his performance went unnoticed.

16. A new era characterized by a number of films, including Sam Peckinpah's *Straw Dogs*, released on the same day as *Dirty Harry* in 1971, the year that also saw the release of Stanley Kubrick's *A Clockwork Orange* and of William Friedkin's *The French Connection*. All these films were the product of a United States traumatized by the televised images of the Vietnam War, the assassinations of Martin Luther King and Robert Kennedy, student unrest, the riots in the predominantly black neighbourhoods of Watts and Newark, and the assassinations of various Black Panther leaders. More and more films began to reflect these events, coming out of a Hollywood that had changed, a whole generation of 'new wave' filmmakers at its helm, freed from the dictates of the Hays Code (censorship) and also influenced by the success of the American counter-culture movement. As a result, films such as *Bonnie and Clyde* (Arthur Penn, 1967) and *Easy Rider* (Dennis Hopper, 1969) blazed the trail.

17. About this unique shot in the film and for a more detailed look at America's new cinema, see Jean-François Rauger, 'Juste avant la nuit (les années 70)', *Cahiers du cinéma*, 462 (December 1992).

18. For instance, Don Siegel's *Two Mules for Sister Sara* (1970) starts like a Leone film, even a pastiche of one (with music by Ennio Morricone), then turns into a story about a supposedly intrepid mercenary (eventually turning into a comedic 'Way of the Cross' for Eastwood) accompanied by a prostitute disguised as a nun (Shirley MacLaine). The film's ending sees the Eastwood character's masculinity undone (tamed?) by the female character. In fact, right from the outset it is clear that she wears the trousers. Exactly the same comment was to be made about Sondra Locke in *The Gauntlet*.

19. From memory and with no attempt at being exhaustive: the liberal amount of beatings he receives (*A Fistful of Dollars* and *Dirty Harry*), a face blistered from the sun (*The Good, the Bad and the Ugly*), an arrow that has to be changed from his shoulder (*Two Mules for Sister Sara*), a dislocated shoulder (*Thunderbolt and Lightfoot*). As for his leg amputated with a saw in *The Beguiled*, this surely counts as the masterpiece of Eastwood's cinematic martyrology.

20. Universal Studio's slowness to promote his films was highlighted even more when he later saw how quickly and efficiently Warner Bros. publicized *Dirty Harry* (1971) and its follow-up, *Magnum Force*, in 1973.

21. As was the case with Alan J. Pakula and his film about the Watergate scandal (*All the President's Men*, 1976), and Stanley Kubrick (*A Clockwork Orange*, 1971; *Barry Lyndon*, 1975).

22. When Blake Edwards, a director of stature, tried to work on one of Eastwood's projects, *City Heat* (1984), he eventually had to throw in the towel – to the detriment of the film.

23. Related to this state of mind, two unforgettable motifs recur in the film: the scar that divides his cheek, representing the divide between America's North and South, and also his internal wound, still bleeding and allowing him no peace. Wales also never stops spitting out the black tobacco that he chews continually – a dark bile that, like a man poisoned, he empties over the whole of creation, both man and animal, the living and the dead.

24. This is a key sequence in the film. The two warriors meet and become blood brothers, cutting their hands in a sign of recognition of each other (alter egos? the same but other?) and mixing their blood. Through this final act of scarring, Wales's original wound is finally healed.

25. And twenty-five years later, the boxing hall in Eastwood's accomplished *Million Dollar Baby* was to also create a similar kind of utopia: an old trainer, an African-American ex-boxer who has become a security guard, a slightly backward orphan nicknamed Danger because he wouldn't hurt a fly, and a young woman alone in the world. Once again a self-created community outside the norm, a sort of reconstituted family that harks back to an inaccessible dream of an America in which the last will be the first …

26. An owl, a snake, a rabbit and a tarantula in the first shots of *Two*

Mules for Sister Sara, the dog adopted by Breezy in the film of the same name, as well as the one who follows Josey Wales, the dogs in *Tightrope*, the bulldog in *Sudden Impact* and another dog in *Midnight in the Garden of Good and Evil*, the famous orangutan, a chimpanzee in *Space Cowboys*, the chickens in the car in *Honkytonk Man*, an African elephant in *White Hunter, Black Heart*, Bronco Billy's horse as well as those belonging to the Pale Rider and William Munny in *Unforgiven*, and so forth. A painting depicting Noah's Ark sits above the childhood bed of Dave (Tim Robbins) in *Mystic River*.

27. Theodor Reik, *The Haunting Melody: Psychoanalytic Experiences in Life and Music*, Farrar, Straus and Young, New York, 1953.

28. Michel Foucault, in a lecture given in 1967, published in 1984 and reprinted in *Dits et écrits II, 1976–88*, Gallimard, Paris, 2001.

29. The success of *Every Which Way But Loose* is a good example. For an original budget of $5 million, the film went on to take $120 million worth of box-office receipts in the United States alone.

30. Warner Bros. was also a stakeholder in Warner Communications, Inc., which would become Time Warner Inc., the most powerful media conglomerate in the world, following its merger with Time Inc. in 1990.

31. For example, the cinematographer Bruce Surtees, the editor Ferris Webster and the production designer Henry Bumstead.

32. For example, Tom Stern became a cinematographer, Joel Cox, an editor, and the career of musician Lennie Niehaus also received support from Eastwood.

33. In January 1979, *La Revue du cinéma* was the first serious journal to dedicate an entire article (around thirty pages) to the man who made *Every Which Way but Loose*…

34. As quoted by Patrick McGilligan (*Clint: The Life and Legend*, St. Martin's Press, New York, 1999, p. 396): 'I'm just now beginning to realize that though Mr Eastwood may have been improving over the years, it's also taken all these years for most of us to recognize his very consistent grace and wit as a filmmaker.'

35. This extraordinary land race, the Cherokee Strip, still resonates as an orgiastic episode in the vast plundering of the Native American tribes by the American state.

36. Eastwood experimented with racism by reversing the image and imagining an American in Africa in *White Hunter, Black Heart* (1990), in order to show that, in spite of his most liberal intentions, western man will only ever be 'a white hunter with a black heart'.

37. In *High Plains Drifter* the vengeful man on horseback forces the inhabitants to paint their entire town red, as if exhuming a memory of the white man and the 'redskin' of America's repressed history.

38. This is undoubtedly the figure of a phantom or reincarnated being: it is the ghost or origin that cannot speak its name, returning because it has been forgotten, demanding reparations for all: the Indian of Oklahoma or the disenfranchised African-American, all those who have been banished yet haunt the edges of America's guilty and amnesiac present.

39. Eastwood always plays these fathers, the most memorable being John 'Thunderbolt' in *Thunderbolt and Lightfoot*, the Honkytonk Man, the cop in *Tightrope*, William Munny (who says, 'You don't have to worry, Kid. I ain't going to kill you. You're the only friend I got'), the thief in *Absolute Power* and the old trainer in *Million Dollar Baby*.

40. Especially as at that time they were not intending to make any more new films with this character.

41. In *Tightrope* (1984) – one of cinematographer Bruce Surtees' masterpieces – Eastwood's character tracks down a serial killer in a New Orleans red-light district, making the film a heterosexual version of William Friedkin's *Cruising* (1980). *Tightrope* is also liberally inspired – if a little timidly so – by Edgar Allan Poe's short story 'William Wilson' (1839), about a man who believed he had a double, until he does in fact meet him in a mirror.

42. 'Cinema is the only thing left that America can still believe in' is the conclusion Marc Chevrie was already making ('Le dernier des cow-boys', *Cahiers du cinéma*, 393, March 1987) when *Heartbreak Ridge* was released. But how could you define 'an end as right as when it started', when what started was called 'Korea' or 'Vietnam'?

43. For example, the scene in *The Good, the Bad and the Ugly* where shots of Blondie (Eastwood) sitting at the table in his hotel room calmly assembling his gun are alternated with ones of his approaching assailants. Blondie finishes preparing his gun just as they arrive and he shoots them.

44. *Brigadoon*: a film, based on a musical, directed by Vincente Minnelli (1954).

45. If you conclude hat Steve Everett (Eastwood), the *Oakland Tribune* journalist, arrived in time to foil the execution, that Frank Beechum rightfully escaped death as a result of the way the film leaves the ending open-ended, then you haven't understood *True Crime* or, in fact, Eastwood's cinema. This time the man on death row has not escaped his fate and Everett, although he has tried to right the past, arrives one minute too late, in the way that it is too late for Butch … Nothing or nobody can stop the reels of this film turning – they are like the hands of a clock ticking or the events of a story moving inexorably towards an unavoidable outcome.

46. At the end of Orson Welles's *Citizen Kane* (1941), we discover that 'Rosebud' – the final word uttered by Kane, the dying tycoon, which has prompted endless speculation ever since – represents his lost childhood.

47. Incidentally, everything was to start happening for Eastwood during this period, including a first contract with Universal Studios.

48. Nicholas Ray, 'Hommage aux cinéphiles' (1978) in Nicholas Ray, Susan Ray, Sylvia Hill, *Action: sur la direction d'acteurs*, Yellow Now/Fémis, Crisnée/Paris, 1992.

49. Omar Khayyam, *Rubaiyat*, excerpt quoted by Charlie Parker in *Bird*.

50. For a history of 'phantomology' or the study of ghosts, see Hélène Boisset, 'Clint Eastwood: la revenance', in Jean-Pierre Moussaron and Jean-Baptiste Thoret (eds), *Why Not? Sur le cinéma américain*, Rouge Profond, Pertuis, 2003.

Sources

Clint Eastwood Collection: p. 49, 94 (1st, 2nd and 4th col.), 95 (1st and 3rd col.). Collection Cahiers du cinéma: inside front cover, 2–3, 4–5, 9, 10, 11, 12, 13, 14, 21, 22, 23, 24–5, 25 (bottom), 26–7, 28 (bottom), 34–5, 40–1, 43, 46–7, 48, 50–1, 52, 55, 56, 57, 58–9, 61, 62–3, 64, 65, 66, 68–9, 70, 71, 72, 73, 74–5, 76–7, 79, 80, 81 (left), 82, 84, 85, 86 (bottom), 86–7, 88, 89, 90–1, 92, 93, 95 (4th col.), 96 (top and center), 97 (1st col. center; 3rd col. top and bottom; 4th col.), 98 (1st col. top and center; 2nd, 3rd and 4th col.), 99, 103, inside back cover.

Collection Cahiers du cinéma/Dominique Rabourdin: p. 30, 32, 33, 42, 97 (1st col. top; 2nd col.).

Collection CAT'S: p. 8, 31, 39, 94 (3rd col.).

Collection Cinémathèque Française: p. 16–7, 18, 44, 97 (1st col. bottom; 3rd col. center).

Collection Cinémathèque Française/BIFI: p. 6, 15.

Corbis Outline: cover.

Screen grabs: p. 19, 20, 28 (top), 29, 36, 37, 54, 60, 78, 81 (right), 98 (1st col. bottom).

Credits

© Arturo Gonzáles Producciones Cinematográficas S.A./Constantin Film Produktion/Produzioni Europee Associati: p. 15, 16–7.

© Avala Film/Katzka-Loeb/MGM: p. 31.

© Castle Rock Entertainment/Columbia Pictures Industry: p. 54, 65, 70, 71, 81 (bottom right), 98 (2nd col. top), inside back cover.

© CBS Entertainment: p. 12, 13.

© Constantin Film Produktion/Ocean Films: p. 6, 14 (top).

© Jennings Lang/Malpaso Company: p. 26–7.

© Leonard Freeman Productions: p. 23.

© Jim McHugh: cover.

© Malpaso Company: p. 44.

© MGM: p. 38.

© Paramount Pictures: p. 28 (bottom).

© Traverso: p. 45.

© Universal Studios Inc.: p. 8, 9, 18, 24–5, 28 (top), 49, 86 (bottom), 86–7, 94 (3rd col.), 96, 99 (1st col. center), 103.

© Vulcan Productions/Reverse Angle International: p. 95 (4th col.).

© Warner Bros Entertainment Inc.: inside front cover, 2–3, 4–5, 10, 11, 19, 20, 21, 22, 25 (bottom), 29, 30, 32, 33, 34–5, 36, 37, 39, 40–1, 42, 46–7, 48, 50–1, 52, 55, 56, 57, 58–9, 60, 61, 62–3, 64, 66, 68–9, 72, 73, 74–5, 76–7, 78, 79, 80, 81 (top and left), 82, 84, 85, 88, 89, 90–1, 92, 93, 97, 98 (1st col.; 2nd col. center and bottom; 3rd and 4th col.), 99 (1st col. top and bottom; 2nd col.).

Acknowledgements

I would particularly like to thank Nicole Brenez, Stéfani de Loppinot, Peggy Hannon, Thierry Horguelin and Jean-Baptiste Thoret.
Thanks also to Laurent Chaine, Bernard Eisenschitz, Charlotte Garson, Christophe Jouanlanne, Ghislaine Lassiaz, Adrian Martin, Jean-François Rauger, Brad Stevens. And, finally, Sylvie, Colette, Frédéric, Alice, Carmen and Valentine.

Opposite page: Clint Eastwood and Angelina Jolie on the set of *Changeling* (2008).
Cover: Clint Eastwood in the early 2000s.
Inside front cover: Clint Eastwood in *Unforgiven* (1992).
Inside back cover: Ed Harris and Clint Eastwood in *Absolute Power* (1997).

Cahiers du cinéma Sarl
65, rue Montmartre
75002 Paris

www.cahiersducinema.com

Revised English edition © 2010 Cahiers du cinéma Sarl
First published in French as *Clint Eastwood* © 2007 Cahiers du cinéma Sarl

ISBN 978 2 8664 2570 8

Series conceived by Claudine Paquot
Designed by Werner Jeker/Les Ateliers du Nord
Translated by Sarah Robertson
Printed in China